THE SEER
in Celtic and Other Traditions

THE SEER
in Celtic and Other Traditions

Edited by
HILDA ELLIS DAVIDSON

JOHN DONALD PUBLISHERS LTD
EDINBURGH

ISBN 0 85976 259 9

Distributed in the United States of America and
Canada by Humanities Press Inc., Atlantic
Highlands, NJ 07716, U.S.A.

Phototypeset by Quorn Selective Repro Ltd., Loughborough.
Printed in Great Britain by Bell & Bain Ltd., Glasgow.

Preface

This book is based on papers given at a symposium on 'The Seer', held at Linacre College, Oxford, in July 1987, through the kind offices of Dr Juliette Wood, and organised on behalf of the Folklore Society. There is a strong Celtic emphasis in the papers and a particular interest in material from Scotland, as might be expected from the chosen theme. The papers in the second part of the book deal with activities of the seer in different parts of the world at various periods, ranging from seers of Ancient Israel and Early China to successful practitioners of the present day in Pakistan and Japan, and offer a valuable basis for comparison.

I should like to take this opportunity to express thanks to all who helped in the organising of the symposium, and especially to Dr Juliette Wood for enabling it to run so smoothly. Thanks are also due to all who contributed papers, and who took part in the stimulating discussions. We are particularly grateful to Mrs Eilidh Watt, who came from Skye to give us a vivid and objective account of her own experiences of the Second Sight, which she has expanded into a paper. I should like to thank Basil Megaw and Professor Karl Hauck for kindly granting permission to reproduce drawings, and Eileen Aldworth for the generous help given with the illustrations. Finally I must thank the publishers, John Donald, for undertaking the production of this book, and for help and advice throughout.

Hilda Ellis Davidson
Cambridge, 1989

Contents

Contents

List of Contributors

DR CARMEN BLACKER

Lecturer in Japanese in the University of Cambridge and formerly President of the Folklore Society. Author of *The Catalpa Bow: a Study of Shamanistic Practices in Japan* et al.

DR HILDA ELLIS DAVIDSON

Formerly Vice-President of Lucy Cavendish College, Cambridge and President of the Folklore Society. Author of *Gods and Myths of Northern Europe* et al.

DR MICHAEL LOEWE

Lecturer in Chinese Studies in the University of Cambridge. Co-Editor of vol.I of the Cambridge History of China. Author of *Chinese Ideas of Life and Death* et al.

DR JOHN MACINNES

Senior Lecturer in the School of Scottish Studies, University of Edinburgh, specialising in Gaelic song poetry.

PROF. JOHN MACQUEEN

Professor of Scottish Literature and Oral Traditions and Director of the School of Scottish Studies, University of Edinburgh.

SAMUEL PYEATT MENEFEE

Fellow of Royal Anthropological Institute and American Anthropological Association. Degrees from Yale, Oxford, Harvard and University of Virginia. Author of *Wives for Sale*, winner of the first Katharine Briggs Prize.

DR VENETIA NEWALL

Honorary Research Fellow in Folklore, University College, London. Visiting Fellow, School of Slavonic Studies, University of London. Honorary Editor, *International Folklore Review*. Formerly President of the Folklore Society.

PROF. the REVD CANON J.R. PORTER
Professor Emeritus of Theology in the University of Exeter. Formerly President of the Society for Old Testament Study and of the Folklore Society.

EILIDH WATT
Native of the Island of Skye. Author and broadcaster in Gaelic.

DR JULIETTE WOOD
Former Research Fellow of the University of Wales. Currently holds a Leverhulme Grant at Linacre College, Oxford, and is preparing a comprehensive Index to Welsh Folk Narrative.

Introduction

Hilda Ellis Davidson

A simple definition of Second Sight is given by Samuel Johnson in his account of the journey he made with James Boswell to the Hebrides in 1773:[1]

> An impression made either by the mind upon the eye, or by the eye upon the mind, by which things distant or future are perceived, and seen as if they were present.

This appears to be based on an earlier account, supported by many examples, by Martin Martin, a gentleman of Skye, published in 1703.[2] Martin travelled in the Western Isles and recorded what he observed of the life of the inhabitants and the features of the landscape. He gave a short paper on strange phenomena there to the Royal Society in 1697,[3] but here makes no mention of the Second Sight. The book produced a few years later, however, dedicated to Prince George of Denmark, contains a long section entitled 'An account of the Second Sight in Irish called Taish', some of which is quoted on p.13f. below. This aroused considerable interest among learned men of the time. Johnson's father gave him a copy in his boyhood, and Boswell borrowed one from the Advocates' Library in Edinburgh to take on their journey; although Johnson thought poorly of Martin as a writer, he had evidently studied him with great thoroughness.[4]

Martin's definition of Second Sight was vaguer than Johnson's, but he goes on to tell much that Johnson does not. Johnson knew no Gaelic, and indeed despised it as 'the rude speech of a barbarous people who had few thoughts to express', so that he was unable to receive information at first hand. 'There is one living in Skye with whom we would have gladly conversed', he informs us, 'but he was very gross and ignorant, and knew no English.' Martin, on the other hand, though in his Royal Society paper he shows himself somewhat naive,[5] was clearly familiar with the phenomenon and witnessed many examples of it.

Johnson wished to find out for himself how far the claims made by Martin and other writers from Scotland were capable of proof, and he satisfied himself that a belief in Second Sight was indeed shared by 'Islanders of all degrees, whether of rank or understanding, except the Ministers, who universally deny it, in consequence of a system against

1

conviction'. He used some of Martin's arguments in refuting their objections. However, he was left with a feeling of uncertainty regarding the Second Sight, since he became increasingly doubtful of the reliability of his informants when their information on other subjects proved inaccurate. He was also rendered uneasy because 'this faculty of seeing things out of sight is local and common useless . . . without any visible reason or perceptible benefit', and because it was mainly 'the mean and ignorant who seemed to possess it'. So he came away in the end without any firm conviction, though 'willing to believe'.

The testimony of Dr Johnson, sensible, downright and honest as it is, shows the difficulties confronting a learned man from a predominantly literary background who sets out to explore evidence which his education and scale of values prevent him from fully appreciating. The kind of proof he and his contemporaries sought was simply not available, and many others since Johnson have been similarly frustrated. Yet he admitted that the firm belief in the powers of the seers was established among educated men in Scotland as well as the simple, and although he met few men of education with such powers, he admitted that 'on such men it has sometimes fallen'.[6] In more civilised parts of Scotland he was assured that the Second Sight 'is wearing away with other superstitions, and that its reality is no longer supposed but by the grossest people', but he could not vouch for this after his journey to the islands.

In this collection of papers, an attempt has been made to consider various manifestations of this strange and irrational power which Johnson calls 'a mode of seeing superadded to that which nature generally bestows'. We begin appropriately with the Scottish Highlands, where records of Second Sight aroused such interest in the seventeenth and eighteenth centuries, and the material presented comes both from recent experience and the remote past. John MacInnes, who has worked on oral literature and popular beliefs in Scotland for many years, and himself comes from a family in which many have possessed the gift, discusses Gaelic traditions concerning seers. His paper contains valuable new material, and he stresses one important factor, the seer's function as a creative artist and 'the products of his visions as art-forms . . . shaped by the expectations of society and its aesthetic needs'. This was a view utterly beyond the comprehension of Johnson in the eighteenth century. Several points in this paper are further illustrated by the evidence of Eilidh Watt, who has herself experienced this 'mode of seeing' since girlhood. Unlike the seers in Skye with whom Johnson failed to communicate, she is both articulate and objective, and one feels that such an honest account of personal experience would have been greatly valued by him. Other papers range from naive examples of Second Sight such as were related to Johnson and

Boswell to claims of more elaborate revelations and impressive powers in various periods and societies.

Scholars of Johnson's time seem to have regarded the Second Sight as something separate from divination and prophecy, in spite of their familiarity with the Bible and the classics. Robert Kirk in *The Secret Commonwealth*, written about 1691, was well aware of Biblical parallels, but his book was not published until 1815, although there were copies in circulation.[7] A distinction may be made between seer and diviner when the seer's visions come suddenly and unsought, as in Martin's account, and no special technique is used to inspire them. Therefore the Scottish seers made no profit from their revelations, and their gift was not considered a valuable one. Johnson shrewdly takes up this point: 'They have no temptation to feign, and their hearers no motive to encourage the imposture'. But this may not always have been the case, since it is natural for people to seek out those thought to possess special knowledge to solve their problems for them, and in many cultures natural seers strive to gain control over their power to see what is hidden, so that they can summon it at will. While it is evident that Eilidh Watt has felt no such urge, Venetia Newall's paper on professional seers among Punjabi immigrants in Britain shows how profitable a business can be built up today by genuine or pretended gifts of this kind. This is backed by advertisements in newspapers, and vast numbers of clients are prepared to pay large sums of money in return for hope of help. An even more surprising manifestation of the possibilities of divination used for healing is that described by Carmen Blacker in her account of the new cult of child embryos in Japan. This has reached enormous proportions in the last few years; she was able to visit one of the new temples where an experienced seer, his powers enhanced by long and arduous training, sees the embryo ghost of a child killed through abortion or miscarriage, who is causing pain and suffering to the parent who denied it life. Women who have had one or more abortions, and are now showing physical or psychosomatic symptoms which doctors cannot cure, throng to the temples to discover how to appease these angry infant ghosts. Many indeed are cured, and such therapy forms part of a larger movement in which resentful ghosts causing suffering to the living in order to draw attention to their plight are identified and appeased. Evidently a sophisticated technical education is not necessarily a hindrance to the acceptance of a belief that certain individuals 'form a bridge of vital importance between our own world and the invisible world'.

Such an approach may be found in widely different cultures. The Celtic saint Columba, whose *Life* was written in the seventh century by Adomnan, is presented in the paper by John MacQueen from this point of view, since Adomnan sees Columba essentially as a seer rather than as a missionary saint, as he appears in Bede's writings. Columba's abilities 'reached across time and space', and he was 'capable of perceiving spiritual as well as physical entities'. When Columba describes where a thief is to be found, crouching under an upturned boat covered with grass among sandhills, there is a preciseness and vividness in the description which may be compared with those claimed to be given by seers in recent times, when for instance they state where a dead body may be found.[8] In Columba we have a seer who, unlike those to whom Johnson refers, was by no means restricted to 'local' visions, and who could also sometimes accurately forecast the time of a coming event. As a saint of God, and one accustomed to move among the leaders of the people, he could foresee such happenings as battles and the fate of royal houses, as well as the futures of individuals. It is noteworthy also that prophecies might be interwoven with accounts of his visions. Sometimes there were limits to his powers of perception, as when the identity of someone seen was not revealed to him, but he was evidently held to possess remarkable powers. These were not felt to be unique to him, however, since a man of God was expected to demonstrate such powers as part of his holiness.

Besides perceiving happenings in the future and at a distance, he could also see invisible beneficent powers, here called angels, and mischievous and destructive ones, here called demons, whose mainly physical activities might be held in check by the potency of his blessing. One of John Aubrey's correspondents claimed that Second Sight in Scotland related only to the future: 'Past Events I learn nothing of it'.[9] Columba, however, was able through the power of the Holy Spirit to behold 'many of the secret things that have been hidden since the world began'. This is said to have happened when he stayed in a darkened house for three days and nights, allowing access to no one. Here is something of a different order from the brief visions vouchsafed to the later Highland seers, and we have within a Christian setting something comparable to the seeking after hidden knowledge in darkness and solitude associated with Celtic and Scandinavian seers in the pre-Christian period.

The special powers possessed by the man of God, putting him in touch with the Other World, are again emphasised in J. R. Porter's study of the seer in Ancient Israel. He discusses the distinction between seer and prophet, although clearly one man might carry out both functions. Samuel, Elijah and Elisha were primarily seers, whereas figures like Amos, Isaiah and Micah are remembered as prophets; in the first case, tales of the seer's actions and achievement are told, while in the second we are given long prophetic utterances in elaborate and often obscure poetic language. The early seers are represented as dealing both with everyday matters and also with affairs of state. Unlike the simple folk known to Martin, these are trained professionals, and as such accept payment for their services. In distinguishing between seer and prophet, the use of different words for seeing may be significant.

The prophet in early Celtic tradition was also a poet, although John MacInnes finds little evidence of this in recent Gaelic oral tradition. The topic is discussed by Juliette Wood in her paper on the prophecies of Merlin and Taliesin in medieval Wales. Here, as with the seers of Israel, folklore is of considerable importance in shaping the tradition. She points out how simple folk beliefs, including the readiness to see omens in nature, can support the growth of prophecy, and how this may be further strengthened by an increase in national consciousness. Prophecy may be a call to action and a political weapon, and again we are far from the naive spontaneous predictions of the Scottish seers, yet the origins are surely the same.

In Ancient China, development from the unskilled amateur to the highly professional prophet and diviner employed as government official seems to have progressed to lengths unequalled elsewhere. This is indicated in Michael Loewe's paper on Chinese prophecy, dealing mostly with evidence before 200 AD. While there are references to 'masters of the Way', who seem to be self-trained seers, these were outnumbered by officials, Government officers responsible for deciding whether a proposed course of action would prove successful. Under such a system, which offered those in power a convenient way to avoid taking the blame for mistakes, various types of divination and oracles developed. This led to increased dependence on standardised methods of consultation rather than individual inspiration and direct vision.

There is little indication in Martin's account of natural seers being taught to develop their gifts, although there are some slight suggestions of this (p.15 below). In Ancient Israel the seer could be installed by his teacher, as in the case of Elisha inheriting the mantle and staff of Elijah. Cloak and staff were a frequent part of the ritual of prophecy, and used by both Celtic and Germanic seers in early times. There must have been many rituals used in the endeavour to learn control of visionary powers and to use them at will. My paper on the Seer's thumb is an attempt to discover whether one simple ritual, the putting of the thumb into the mouth, was once deliberately employed as a method of gaining inspiration. The gesture is emphasised in the literature, art and folklore of both Ireland and the Scandinavian colonies in England, as well as in Scandinavia itself. There certainly seems no doubt that use of parts of the body formed an important part in the seer's training, and that the power to see might be transmitted by touch.

The vision of a funeral passing down a road or entering the churchyard, sometimes by an unfamiliar route, was widely held to be a reliable portent that a real funeral would shortly pass that way. Such premonitions of death are reported from the seventeenth century in Scotland, and Johnson comments in his characteristic way: 'That they should often see death is to be expected, because death is an event frequent and important'. Another well-established sign of approaching death was the appearance of a shroud or winding-sheet enveloping a living person. Robert Kirk describes this gradually creeping up to the head:[10]

> . . . till it came to the knee, and afterwards it came up to the middle, then to the shoulders, and at last over the head, which was visible to no other person . . . when it approached his head, he told that such a person was ripe for the grave.

This tradition continued in Skye, for Eilidh Watt heard her father announce that he had seen the death veil shrouding his sister, and knew that she had only a short while to live. Such a knowledge of approaching death, often to a relative or friend, may be one reason why we are continually told that the Second Sight was a burden to those possessing it, and many longed to be delivered from it. 'It's commonly talk'd by all I spoke with, That it is troublesome and they would gladly be freed from it, but cannot', wrote one of Aubrey's correspondents.[11] Another possible reason is suggested by Eilidh Watt's account of the terrifying sensation of overwhelming evil which she once endured, since a seer is vulnerable to destructive spiritual influences as well as beneficent ones. Even with disciplined control, the power of Second Sight could evidently be painful, and to make the considerable effort needed to obtain a revelation on demand is generally represented as both hard and dangerous.

A particular development of the phantom funeral found over a large part of England and Wales was the custom of sitting up in the church porch or outside the church, particularly on St Mark's Eve but also on certain other nights, to watch for the procession of those doomed to die in the next twelve months. Sam Menefee in his paper gives an astonishing number of references to this practice, which continued from the seventeenth century until almost the end of Victoria's reign. Occasionally the happier sight of couples walking arm in arm was seen, indicating marriages within the year, but these were in the minority. Those who watched are sometimes called 'fortune-tellers'. There are many cautionary tales of bold young people watching out of a spirit of adventure, and of how such rash individuals paid dearly for their audacity. So widespread a practice must have been prevalent earlier in England, and may have developed out of the belief in the phantom funeral and taken this particular form after the Reformation. Sam Menefee points out significant links with folklore which strengthened the tradition and kept it alive.

The involuntary seeing of what is invisible to normal sight has clearly continued over the centuries, developing in different ways according, as John MacInnes points out, to the expectations and needs of society. Much depended on how far the gift was recognised and supported by the established religious organisation. Johnson found obstinate disbelief among ministers of the Scottish church whom he met, who were determined to deny any claims to Second Sight as due to superstition and deceit. This, however, was by no means the case everywhere in the Highlands, since we have the sympathetic picture given by Robert Kirk and Frazer of Tiree, among others. In Adomnan's time the church evidently found nothing to condemn in the gift of foreknowledge, since this formed part of the powers expected to be possessed by a saint. The testimony of Ancient Israel is similar, and provides Biblical precedent; while it was forbidden to consult the Witch of Endor, who was seeking unlawful knowledge from the lower world, it was praiseworthy to listen to seers such as Samuel or Elijah, chosen by the Lord to reveal his will to men. Today there are ministers in the islands who themselves possess the Second Sight; some apparently take it for granted, 'of no more consequence than having a talent for music or handicraft' (p.26 below), and they may make use of it to help those in their care. On the other hand, those who find the gift an intolerable burden may turn to the church to be freed from it, as was the case in Aubrey's time (p.25 below). Eilidh Watt tells us that the modern practice of doing this by turning over the pages of a Bible while a minister prays is a means of evoking the power of God represented by his Word when it is felt that the gift is something undesirable.

In this small group of papers, it is only possible to touch on a few aspects of a wide and complex subject, and to trace some lines of development from the simple recognition of the ability of certain people to see what is normally hidden, prevalent in the Highlands of Scotland in the seventeenth and eighteenth centuries. The deliberate fostering of such an ability is clearly difficult to achieve unless recognised methods of training are available, as in Japan. Even without such training, the interest in such powers continues, and among the influences fostering this, folklore plays an important part. One aspect which has not been discussed here is the ability to 'dream true', which has long been recognised in Iceland and continues to be taken seriously there.[12] Johnson saw a link between dreams and the Second Sight, pointing out with his usual perspicacity: 'It involves no more difficulty than dreams, or perhaps the regular exercise of the cogitative faculty'; he also realised that the tradition of Second Sight in the Highlands 'implies only the local frequency of a power which is nowhere totally unknown'. Something at least of the richness and variety of the manifestations of this power has been conveyed in the studies which are presented here.

NOTES

1. Samuel Johnson, *Journey to the Western Islands of Scotland (1775)*, ed. J. D. Fleeman (Oxford, 1985), 89. Subsequent quotations from Johnson are taken from this section of his book.

2. Martin Martin, *Description of the Western Islands of Scotland* (1703), ed. D. J. Macleod (Stirling, 1934).

3. *Trans.Roy.Soc.*, 19: Oct., 1697 (New York 1963), 727.

4. Fleeman's Commentary (note 1), 151, note 1. For Johnson's use of Martin, see T. Jemielty, 'Samuel Johnson, the Second Sight, and his Sources', *Stud.Eng.Lit.* (Rice Univ., Houston), 14 (1974), 403–20.

5. His observations vary from bird behaviour and folk medicine to a reference to a boy on Skye who could 'erect his ears at will'.

6. Johnson alluded to one gentleman with the gift who complained of its effects, but does not seem to have met him (Fleeman, note 1 above, 212, note 2).

7. Robert Kirk, *The Secret Commonwealth*, ed. S. Sanderson (Mistletoe Books 5, Folklore Society, 1976), 64ff.

8. E.g. N. Macrae, *Highland Second Sight* (Dingwall, n.d.? 1908), quoting from *Rowan Tree Annual*, 1907–8, gives an account of Rachel Macgregor in the Rannoch Hills revealing where the body of a drowned man could be found (103ff.).

9. J. Aubrey, *Miscellanies* (*Three Prose Works*, ed. J. Buchanan-Brown, Fontwell, 1972), 113, from first letter of Aubrey's 'learned friend'.

10. R. Kirk (note 7), 60.

11. J. Aubrey (note 9), 115.

12. H. E. Davidson, 'The Germanic World', *Divination and Oracles*', ed. M. Loewe and C. Blacker (1981), 115.

I. THE CELTIC SEER

Among the early Celtic peoples the inculcation of poetic inspiration and the entire mantic art were developed and elaborated to a degree for which we know no parallel.

N. K. Chadwick, *Poetry nd Prophecy* (1941)

1

The Seer in Gaelic Tradition

John MacInnes

One of the words for 'poet' in Gaelic is *fili*.[1] According to accepted opinion, it is connected with the root of a verb 'to see': the *fili* was originally a seer. From this one might be led to suppose that poetry and prophecy, or divination in general, are closely linked in Gaelic tradition; the more so as romantic notions still persist in some quarters, of the Gaelic bard with his 'eye in a fine frenzy rolling.' In actual fact, the figure of the 'seer-poet' has very little place either in the historical record or in the oral tradition of Gaelic. In Scots Gaelic, to which this short account is restricted, there is indeed a very important prophecy which is ascribed to a particular poet and alluded to by other poets and I shall deal with it at the end of the chapter. There are also occasional stray verses, some of which can be regarded as a sub-class of the lore of names, that presage death or disaster at a certain place, as in the following stanza from the Isle of Skye, which I give in translation. *Tobar Tà* is a well in the parish of Strath:

> Tobar Tà, that well Tobar Tà
> A well at which a battle will be fought
> Lachlan of the three Lachlans will be slain
> Early, early at Tobar Tà.

Lachlan is a common personal name among the MacKinnons in whose traditional territory the well of Tobar Tà lies. But there is a variant which substitutes the personal name Torcall, traditionally a MacLeod name and in particular the eponym of *Siol Torcaill*, the Seed of Torcall, who are the MacLeods of Lewis and their derivative kindreds. It has been suggested that this variant refers to the death of Torcall who was the third Torcall of the Lewis line; his sister married Lachlan MacKinnon of Strath and Torcall MacLeod may have met his death in MacKinnon territory through having come to Skye for refuge or aid.[2] Such prophecies are on this analysis all *ex post facto*. But even to the present day they are not so regarded in Gaelic tradition. Like most prophecies they are ambiguous with a fine protean quality — a third version declares that *torc nan trì lochan*, 'the

10

boar of the three lochs', will be killed at Tobar Tà — and their fulfilment is still awaited by some people.

It may be that such rhymes are vestiges of a tradition of poetic prophecy, but to go beyond that would be most unsafe in the light of the evidence at our disposal. It would also be inappropriate, in my opinion, in the present context, to enquire whether any of these predictions, so-called, are the expression of anything that might be described as genuine precognition. We do better to accept them here as cultural items which have their place in the social construction of reality. Traditional Gaelic culture in Scotland presents us with a strong sense of territory in which place-names are charged with historical and legendary associations in a timeless order in which geography and history are merged. On such a plane, our modern divisions of time into past, present and future may not, for the makers of these 'prophetic' rhymes, have had the relevance that we are so much inclined to take for granted. However that may be, the prophecies themselves have survived in Gaelic into the modern age where such temporal divisions do obtain. And in modern Gaelic there exist other beliefs also that clearly are tied to the notion of linear time, the most conspicuous being the concept of Second Sight. In fact it is not too much to say that in contemporary Gaelic society, the very idea of divination is centred on the belief in Second Sight.

In earlier times there was a greater range of techniques at people's disposal both for revealing future events and for describing present events happening at a distance. We can still hear in tradition about some of the mechanisms of these arts just as we can hear, more immediately, of isolated visions, waking or dreaming, that fall in our own day and involve precognition and detection. These latter experiences may not always be classed as instances of Second Sight but in so far as people actually give them credence, it is because they relate them to this pivotal phenomenon of Second Sight. Gaelic society accepts, if one may put it that way, that certain individuals exist who have peculiar clairvoyant powers which are not subject to the control of the will. It is accepted too that any of us may have premonitions or similar experiences — perhaps only once in a lifetime — and, equally, that any of us may be misled as to the nature of such experiences. It is in fact not unusual to hear it said that So-and-So, who claimed to have had a precognitive vision, was more likely to have been day-dreaming or had succumbed to some form of self-indulgent fantasy. But that is very different from denying the existence of Second Sight itself. Second Sight is not a form of self-indulgence; more often than not it is regarded as an affliction; and, moreover, it is a faculty whose existence is endorsed by the two great forces of authority that validate experience in a traditional society: the powers of the non-mortal world and the testimony of the ancestors. And so, if we do accept someone's claim regarding an isolated vision or premonition, it is because at the centre of this cosmology, the idea of Second Sight is so firmly established.

Within the same frame of reference, we explain other phenomena. For instance, I have on several occasions heard discussions on belief in the existence of fairies summed up by the observation that the capacity to see the fairies must have been a form of Second Sight now lost to us.

With regard to all these matters there are of course sceptics or at least those who profess scepticism. But overall I think one might say that such sceptics are no more than agnostic. At the same time we must not assume we can measure degree of belief by the popularity of stories about Second Sight. Many of these stories survive simply because they are vivid narratives and those who keep them in circulation may well be the most sceptical, while those who are held to have Second Sight themselves are often the most reticent. But there is evidence that that was not always so.

The English term 'Second Sight' is on record from the seventeenth century, all the early references being in Highland contexts. Nevertheless, 'Second Sight' is not a direct translation from Gaelic: the Gaelic term is *An Dà Shealladh*, literally 'the two sights'; or, much less commonly, *An Dà Fhradharc*, 'the two visions'. (The first is the object of sight; the second is the power of sight.) By the beginning of the eighteenth century the term 'Second Sight' is well established in English usage in ethnographic writings about the Highlands and Islands. These accounts provide a remarkable range of data which makes it plain that the seers of the past were much less inhibited in describing their experiences than their modern counterparts. It would at all events be impossible, in my estimation, to record such astonishing abundance of first-hand reports nowadays. One can think of several reasons for this. In the period to which these testimonies belong, and perhaps in most places until the early years of the twentieth century, the modern sceptical intellect had scarcely begun to impinge on traditional Gaelic society. Even if certain of the writers who took down the evidence profess their own scepticism — few in fact do — their attitudes would not in themselves have had much effect on their informants. The reticence of contemporary seers, on the other hand, is in some degree at any rate due to a fear of being regarded as 'primitive' or 'superstitious'. But it may also be true that the contemporary second-sighted individual actually has less to tell. If we allow that an element of creative imagination is an essential component of divination, we might suggest that certain of the functions of the seer in older, traditional society have been taken over by the creative writers of modern society. I am implying, then, that the seer is an artist and that the products of his vision are art-forms (whatever else they may or may not be) shaped by the expectations of society and its aesthetic needs. Even some of the eighteenth-century writers declare that the visionary faculty is already in decay. Similar statements are, it is true, made about the decay of the traditional arts of Gaelic society in general in the same period, but we cannot use the one set of judgments to invalidate the others.

A parallel can be drawn with the history of Gaelic song. On the verge of extinction in the eighteenth century, according to certain writers of the time, it is still, as modern collectors point out, enjoying an apparently undiminished vigour. But, in fact, the range has diminished; certain metrical and melodic categories have disappeared, displaced in popularity by other forms, and even within the last fifty years individual repertoires have shrunk drastically. The true oral song-maker has virtually gone while the song-writer and the literate poet have taken his place. And much the same could be said of Gaelic story-telling. These are processes of decay but they are also processes of substitution and adaptation. In all of these fields we can reconstruct the main lines of the tradition from our contemporary evidence and in some cases even supplement the data from the past. What we cannot do is readily assemble a comparably rich and varied body of material or recover the authoritative tone of these informants of long ago. But so far as accounts of Second Sight are concerned, I know of nothing from one period that absolutely contradicts our information from the other.

As in contemporary Gaelic society, occasional experiences were fitted into a frame of reference organised by the concepts of Second Sight and the uniquely endowed Seer. Both in past and present accounts there is some uncertainty as to whether the faculty is hereditary or may be learned. Before I comment on that and other points, let me quote from a celebrated description written by Martin Martin (c.1660–1719), a native of the Isle of Skye. A number of the observations he makes can be compared with the testimony of modern tradition. Martin, a graduate in medicine of Edinburgh and Leyden, was a keen and intelligent observer of his Gaelic community and no sceptic in regard to the existence of Second Sight:

> THE Second Sight is a singular faculty of seeing an otherwise invisible object, without any previous means used by the person that sees it for that end; the vision makes such a lively impression upon the Seers, that they neither see nor think of any thing else, except the vision, as long as it continues: and then they appear pensive or jovial, according to the object which was represented to them.
>
> At the sight of a vision, the eye-lids of the person are erected, and the eyes continue staring until the object vanish. This is obvious to others who are by, when the persons happen to see a vision, and occurred more than once to my own observation, and to others that were with me.

There is one in Sky, of whom his acquaintance observed, that when he sees a vision, the inner part of his eyelids turn so far upwards, that after the object disappears, he must draw them down with his fingers, and sometimes employs others to draw them down, which he finds to be the much easier way.

This faculty of the Second Sight does not lineally descend in a family, as some imagine, for I know several parents who are endowed with it, but their children not, *et vice versa:* neither is it acquired by any previous compact. And after a strict inquiry, I could never learn from any among them, that this faculty was communicable any way whatsoever.

The Seer knows neither the object, time, nor place of a vision, before it appears. . . .

One instance was lately foretold by a Seer that was a novice, concerning the death of one of my acquaintance; this was communicated to a few only, and with great confidence : I being one of the number, did not in the least regard it, until the death of the person about the time foretold, did confirm me of the certainty of the prediction. The novice mentioned above, is now a skilful Seer. . . .

Children, horses, and cows, see the Second Sight, as well as men and women advanced in years. . . .

That horses see it, is likewise plain from their violent and sudden starting, when the rider or Seer in company with him sees a vision of any kind, night or day. It is observable of the horse, that he will not go forward that way, until he be led about at some distance from the common road, and then he is in a sweat.[3]

Some of the detail in that account finds corroboration in modern tradition, some does not. I have heard references to the staring eyes of the seer but nothing about the turning inwards of the eyelids. There is no longer a belief that children *qua* children 'see the Second Sight', as Martin puts it; nor are cows regarded as being especially sensitive. It is perhaps curious that Martin does not mention dogs: in modern Gaelic society, as in some other cultures, dogs are held to be particularly quick to react to atmosphere, and especially to psychic phenomena. But the horse is unique. Only certain humans are second-sighted; all horses have the faculty. The horse is the Seer of the animal kingdom. Moreover, a horse sees living people in a unique perspective: seven times their real size. If they were not constrained by this peculiar vision, it is said, they would not submit to human domination.

Martin has several references to novice seers, and to one 'that was a novice . . . and . . . is now a skilful Seer'. This implies that the skill develops, though it is not explained what the process of development entails. He provides no information about, for example, initiation or tuition of novices by master seers, for the faculty itself, so far as he could discover, is not 'communicable any way whatsoever'. Nor is it (necessarily) hereditary.

But other witnesses differ somewhat on certain of these points. For instance, in a letter to John Aubrey, dated 1694, the writer declares that 'I am informed, that in the Isle of Sky . . . several families had it by succession, descending from parents to children, and as yet there be many there that have it that way. . . .' And in the same letter Aubrey's correspondent tells of a meeting between his own father and one John MacGrigor, a seer, 'My father . . . being very intimate with the man, told him he would fain learn it [i.e. Second Sight]: to which he answered, that indeed he could in three days time teach him if he pleased; but yet he would not advise him nor any man to learn it; for had he once learned, he would never be a minute of his life but he would see innumerable men and women night and day round about him; which perhaps he would think wearisome and unpleasant, for which reason my father would not have it . . . I am also informed by one who came last summer from the Isle of Sky, that any person that pleases will get it taught him for a pound or two of tobacco.'[4]

Modern tradition has something to say about both points of view. First, the faculty of foreseeing is on the whole hereditary but does not necessarily manifest itself in every individual in a family nor even in every generation. Secondly, it is communicable, temporarily or permanently. The essential element in communication is physical contact.[5] We hear of a seer in the act of seeing, inadvertently or deliberately touching, or being touched by, another person who then shares in the experience. When the contact is broken, participation in the vision ceases immediately. A more elaborate device requires the would-be participant to hold the seer's hand while placing a foot on his foot and looking over his shoulder. There are variants of this stance but in most of the descriptions the left hand or foot or shoulder is involved. In that sense alone, it is a 'sinister' ritual. In some instances this ritual confers only a temporary power, more or less brief; in other instances the faculty remains, although apparently only for the lifetime of the initiated person. In other words, from an evolutionary point of view, it is only an acquired characteristic.

The emphasis on heredity is exceedingly strong in Gaelic society and is used to explain personal qualities, artistic abilities, mannerisms and the like. The possession of Second Sight is fitted into this framework and validated by the concept of hereditary transmission just as the concept of Second Sight itself validates other phenomena. When Martin Martin says: 'several parents are endowed with it, but their children not, *et vice versa* . . .' this would only mean to us that the talent does not manifest itself in every generation. Martin's ideas of heredity are in fact more rigorous than those to which modern Gaelic society subscribes.

There is an anecdote which makes an interesting comment on the relevance of hereditary powers. There were two men working together, the older of whom was a seer. For a long time the younger man pestered his companion to make him a seer too but the older man refused. Eventually, however, he agreed and the younger man became a seer himself. But because Second Sight was not hereditary in his family, he was unable to cope with his experiences and in the end lost his reason.

This suggests that the seer's visions are normally of a tragic nature. In modern tradition this is certainly the case, although one hears of visions that were taken to presage disaster but in the event (which was interpreted as the fulfilment of the vision) produced a happier outcome. None the less, the typical modern vision is the funeral procession. As for times past, our commentators are not unanimous. John Aubrey's informant declares that 'the objects of this knowledge, are not only sad and dismal; but also joyful and prosperous: thus they foretell of happy marriages, good children, what kind of life men shall live, and in what condition they shall die: and riches, honour, preferment, peace, plenty and good weather'.[6]

On premonitions in general, Martin observes that 'Things also are foretold by smelling, sometimes as follows. Fish or flesh is frequently smelled in a fire. . . . This smell several people have, who are not endowed with the Second Sight, and it is always accomplished soon after'.[7]

There is nothing sinister here: merely a foretoken of a certain kind of food. Such prognostications are still believed in and have their own terminology: *manadh, meanmhain, sgrìob*, etc. They may involve any of the senses (smell, curiously enough, least of all, so far as my information goes) and have specific interpretations: an itchy palm signifies one is to get money; the sensation of wispy material in the mouth means drink, and so on. *Manadh* is a more serious portent, generally speaking, and its commonest form is some kind of light. Second-sighted people are held to experience these more frequently than others; and although the seer by definition *sees*, habitual experiences of a non-visual kind may set a person apart from the rest of society. There is perhaps one exception to this in the case of *seinn-bàis*, the 'death-music', a high-pitched humming which portends the death of someone known personally or connected with the family or local community or sometimes even an individual of national standing but who is not an acquaintance. Apparently one can hear the *seinn-bàis* very frequently without acquiring the reputation of a seer.

Dreams are an important vehicle of divination as they are in other cultures. I shall only touch on one aspect of dream interpretation here: the significance of animals in dreams. There was apparently a system in which certain animals represented clans or clan names. Thus a dog represented a MacDonald, a bull a Maclean and a deer a MacKenzie. Sometimes the animal is the same as the animal represented in the clan crest: for instance, the boar for the Campbells. But at least as often, the emblematic animal is different from the dream animal: the crest of the MacLeods shows a bull's head; in dream lore the MacLeods are represented by a horse. It is of great interest that in some Gaelic songs (the examples are seventeenth-century MacDonald compositions and hostile to the MacLeods) the MacLeods are referred to as the 'Seed of the Mare'. These references to the equine ancestry of the MacLeods were taken by themselves as highly insulting, and the choice of another animal, the bull, as their emblem was no doubt deliberate. Behind all this may lie an ancient totemic system.

Stories of dreamers being able to locate a missing person, more often than not a dead person, are well known. Sometimes the dreamer hears a voice, perhaps the voice of the missing person, with or without the appearance of the person, directing the searchers to a particular location. This form of divination, in which events not of the future but of the present, and happening at a distance, could be described, was practised through formal rituals. In the Hebrides the term for this — the word is still known — is *frith; a' deanamh frith'*: 'making a *frith*'. Alexander Carmichael has the following note: 'The 'frith', augury, was a species of divination enabling the 'frithir', augurer, to see into the unseen. This divination was made to ascertain the position and condition of the absent and the lost, and was applied to man and beast. The augury was made on the first Monday of the quarter and immediately before sunrise. The augurer, fasting, and with bare feet, bare head, and closed eyes, went to the doorstep and placed a hand on each jamb. Mentally beseeching the God of the unseen to show him his quest and to grant him his augury, the augurer opened his eyes and looked steadfastly straight in front of him. From the nature and position of the objects within his sight, he drew his conclusions'.[8]

To this I would add, from my own knowledge, that *frith* normally involved bird augury, *a' leughadh nan eun*: 'reading/interpreting the birds'. In some Hebridean dialects, *ealta* 'bird flock', with an interesting semantic shift, seems to be involved in a phrase such as *Tha droch coltas air an ealtainn*: 'The sky looks ominous'. In fact, *ealtainn* can be used in these dialects, without any particular connotation, simply for 'sky'. If my etymology is valid, the link would seem to be provided by the practice of taking auguries from the flight of birds. Another tradition, which I cannot explore here, involves learning of future events from the speech of birds. This happens usually not be design but by chance or good fortune.

Divination by means of the shoulder-blade, the scapula, was widespread throughout the whole Gaelic area and known, of course, in other parts of the world also. There are numerous references to it in our ethnographic literature. Alexander Carmichael again: 'It required highly specialised gifts on the part of the diviner'. In the eighteenth century, John Ramsay of Ochtertyre tells us that 'The scapula or shoulder-blade of a black one-year old sheep is commonly preferred. . . . The moon must not change between the death of the creature and the making this use of its shoulder-blade. . . . In later [*sic*] times a certain proportion of the shoulder-blade was appropriated to every clan'.[9]

This last observation reminds us of the representation of clan names in dreams; while in connection with the scapula again another writer talks of the 'death of some remarkable person in a particular tribe or family'. The ritual was used both for prognosticating the future and for detecting events at a distance. Used for foretelling, it could apparently be fraught with danger for the diviner. At any rate I have heard it said myself that divination from the scapula could put a soul in mortal peril: at a certain point the diviner had to 'go very near the Devil's tooth': *glé fhaisg air fiacaill an Diabhail*.

There is another and rather obscure tradition about locating missing persons. My information can be summarised as follows. Long ago, if a ship failed to return, a certain ritual was carried out. A specially selected woman, who was a virgin, went to sleep and while she slept her spirit left her body and searched for the ship. The woman had to be of strong mind. If the wind changed while her spirit was absent from her body, she was in peril of losing her reason: hence the necessity of having a woman of strong mind. When her spirit returned to her body she woke up and reported where the ship, or its wreckage, was to be found and what had happened to the people aboard. (The changing of the wind may be compared with the detail about divination from the scapula during one phase of the moon.) The description of the search for the ship by the sleeping woman's spirit is suggestive of shamanic trance.

There are several accounts of the progress of a battle being seen in the sky. One of these tells how some women, standing on the Bridge of Inveraray, witnessed the Battle of Ticonderoga, on 10th May 1773, during the American War of Independence, and were able to tell who had been killed or wounded of the soldiers from Argyll, long before the news came by a more conventional route.

The term *An Dà Shealladh* does not nowadays in the North-West Highlands and in the Isles embrace the idea of detection of things at a physical distance. But in the central Highlands, at least from Lochaber to Perthshire, *An Dà Shealladh* includes both precognition and telecognition. Returning to Martin Martin in the Isle of Skye, however, it would appear that the connotation of Second Sight was not so restricted there at the end of the seventeenth century as it is now. At all events, Martin says: 'I have been seen thus myself by Seers of both sexes at some hundred miles distance; some that saw me in this manner, had never seen me personally, and it happened according to their visions, without any previous design of mine to go to those places, my coming there being purely accidental'.

Such manifestations are explained rather differently by modern exponents of the matter. There is a widely distributed belief (which is known also in the Gaelic community of Cape Breton in Canada) that holds that anyone, seer or not, may see the fetch or 'resemblance' of a living person, especially, though not necessarily, if that person feels or expresses an intense desire to visit a particular place or company. What may be an extension or refinement of this is the belief in the existence of a 'co-walker', a *doppelgänger*. If there is a difference between the two notions, it centres on the belief that the 'co-walker' is apt at any given time to be roaming around unknown to its 'owner', creeping up on people in order to frighten them, and generally behaving in a disorderly manner. To that degree, the 'co-walker' is not so much an exact replica of a person as an alternative personality of a much more anarchic nature. Just as a seer may see himself or herself (normally a presage of the seer's death), so anyone may see his or her own 'co-walker', who is recognisable even at a distance because it moves as a mirror-image of the watcher. But there are further variations on this theme. Martin tells of a Lewisman who 'is much haunted by a spirit, appearing in all points like to himself; and he asks many impertinent questions of the man when in the fields, but speaks not a word to him at home, though he seldom misses to appear to him every night in the house, but to no other person. He told this to one of his neighbours, who advised him to cast a live coal at the face of the vision the next time he appeared: the man did so next night, and all the family saw the action; but the following day the same spirit appeared to him in the fields, and beat him severely, so as to oblige him to keep his bed for the space of fourteen days after'.[10]

Before I comment on that, I must look very briefly at some Gaelic terms. The basic word for a 'phantasm' is *taidhbhse*: it is used also for the faculty of seeing phantasms. Etymologically it means something revealed, an appearance or vision. A person with Second Sight is a *taidhbhsear* or, in some dialects, *taidhbhseadar; taidhbhsearachd* is the activity and craft of a seer. In the older English-language accounts of Second Sight, these are the terms that are used should there be any reference to Gaelic terminology.

A fetch or double in the sense of 'astral body' is *samhla*, 'likeness, resemblance'; the *doppelgänger* is *co-choisiche*, literally 'co-walker'. In some areas *samhla* not *taidhbhse* is the word in common use for what might in English be called a ghost, while in others the word *co-choisiche* does not appear to be known at all. 'Ghost' in the sense of 'revenant' does not have much part — certainly not a central part — in the cosmology of Second Sight. Yet there is an adage that both living and dead have a *taidhbhse*. This, however, exists side by side with an adage that only the living has a *taidhbhse*.

In some instances my evidence may be rather fragmentary but my impression is that we are dealing not with one static system of belief but with several dynamic systems. There is certainly no reason to doubt the possibility that change and adaptation have been, and still are, occurring. I am myself inclined to think that the terms *An Dà Shealladh* and *An Dà Fhradharc* are both relatively modern coinages although their exact linguistic relationship with 'Second Sight' presents a difficult problem. *Co-choisiche* has all the appearance of a calque and, indeed, translates '*doppelgänger*'. Yet the essential idea of *doppelgänger* is already present in our specific sense of *samhla*, unequivocally a native term. As I have said earlier, the *co-choisiche* is not so much a replica as an anarchic alternative personality. This is taken a step further (though not chronologically) in the seventeenth century story of the Lewisman who was confronted with his own hostile alter ego. In these connections, one cannot but think of Jekyll and Hyde or of Gilmartin[11] in Hogg's *Confessions of a Justified Sinner*.

Looking at the problem from another angle, it is noteworthy that although Irish and Scots Gaelic culture are fundamentally so similar, neither the terminology of the 'Two Sights' and the 'co-walker' nor the idea of the alternative personality are to be found, so far as I have been able to discover, in genuine Irish Gaelic tradition. It would seem that we are dealing here with a distinctively Scottish concept.

The Lewisman's 'double', you will remember, asked him 'impertinent questions'. Dialogue between a seer and a *taidhbhse* is not unknown although it must be said that modern *taidhbhsean* seem to be notably taciturn. Yet one informant told me of a famous seer in the Hebrides who died around the turn of the century and who was so well acquainted with his *taidhbhsean*, and they with him, that they habitually came into whatever house he happened to be visiting after dark and plucked at his sleeve. He would thereupon rise and go outside to talk to them. (Again, one may compare the Lewisman's spirit who spoke to him 'in the fields'.) But this Hebridean seer always spoke to his ghostly visitants lying prone on the ground: without that contact with the earth he would be in danger.

In the majority of cases, the seer's visions simply fade from perception. I have heard, however, of one seer in Skye, in the late nineteenth century who maintained that the figures disappeared from the ends. Perhaps a variant of the latter mode of seeing is implicit in the account of the death of Donald MacCrimmon the piper during the Jacobite Rising of 1745, when a seer reported 'that, after the said Donald, a goodly person, six feet high, parted with him . . . he saw him all at once contracted to the bigness of a boy of five or six years old, and immediately with the next look, resume his former size'.

Assuming that there has been continuity as well as innovation in what we call Second Sight, it would seem reasonable to suggest that the influence of Christianity would have caused structural changes in the system of belief. During some periods the clergy were fairly lax in their attitudes towards these matters. Still, any system of divination is bound to attract the attention of theologians; in Gaelic society there has clearly been an ambivalent relationship between the Church, in all its branches, and the second-sighted. Some of the early accounts stress the piety of certain seers; others tell of those 'that have a sense of God and religion, and may be presumed to be godly, [who] are known to have this faculty. This evidently appears, in that they are troubled for having it, judging it a sin, that it came from the devil, and not from God; earnestly desiring and wishing to be rid of it, if possible; and to that effect, have made application to their minister, to pray to God for them that they might be exonered from that burden. They have supplicated the presbytery, who judicially appointed public prayers to be made in several churches, and a sermon preached to that purpose, in their own parish church, by their minister; and they have compeared before the pulpit, after sermon, making confession openly of that sin, with deep sense on their knees; renounced any such gift or faculty which they had to God's dishonour, and earnestly desired the minister to pray for them; and this their recantation recorded; and after this, they were never troubled with such a sight any more'.[12]

Modern tradition corroborates this to some extent, telling of the loss of the faculty due to religious conversion, or how seers will only go out at night if they carry a Bible, or how the act of seeing can be terminated by the 'wind of the Bible' (*gaoth a' Bhìobaill*): the draught of air caused by snapping a Bible shut behind the seer's head. At the same time, there is a sanctified precognition: the Rev. John Morrison (1701–1774), the 'Seer of Petty' (a parish near Inverness), and the Rev. Lachlan MacKenzie of Lochcarron (1754–1819) were two of the most celebrated clergymen-seers.

Gaelic oral tradition has also preserved the names of several seers who are not second-sighted men and women gifted or burdened with that particular faculty, but are represented as individuals who deliberately sought to possess occult powers or had them conferred upon them in a special set of circumstances. Certain sinister rituals, like raising the Devil in the form of a monstrous cat, are also alluded to, both in written and oral accounts; although not, so far as I am aware, in genuine oral tradition, in connection with any of these notable people. A seer in this category is not so much a *taidhbhsear* as a *fiosaiche*; his or her occult knowledge is *fiosachd*; (*fios* 'knowledge': the two terms have the appropriate agental and abstract endings). Two of the most celebrated of them were the Lady of Lawers in Perthshire and the *Fiosaiche Ileach* (the Islay Seer).

But the archetypal seer of Gaelic tradition is Coinneach Odhar (Sallow Kenneth), known in English since 1896, when a book of his 'Prophecies' was published, as the 'Brahan Seer', after Brahan Castle, a MacKenzie stronghold in Ross-shire. According to the legend, his mother was given a diviner's stone for him, when he was a baby, by the ghost of a Norse princess in Lewis. In an outstanding piece of historical detective work,[13] the Rev. William Matheson has shown that Coinneach Odhar was a historical character, though not, as had hitherto been supposed, a MacKenzie, who flourished in the 1570s and was probably put to death for sorcery. The legend of Coinneach Odhar was brought from Ross-shire to Lewis, where his birthplace became fixed: carried to the Hebrides, Matheson thinks, through the MacKenzies' conquest of Lewis in the early seventeenth century; and round his name has gathered almost every species of prophecy in Gaelic tradition. Among these are variants of the widespread Signs of the Last Days: women will lose their modesty and ministers will be without Grace.

There is still a lively interest in interpreting the prophecies ascribed to him; his prediction of the coming of the 'black rain', for example, is taken to mean either North Sea oil or alternatively acid rain. And clearly, new prophecies are still being constructed. Quite recently I was told that Coinneach Odhar had predicted that when two women rule this land the kingdom is approaching its end. Some of his older prophecies, about the Clearances, for instance, are ascribed in variant form to other seers also, among them Thomas the Rhymer.

Tómas Reumair, as he is known in Gaelic, has a unique status as prophet of the messianic hope of the Gaels: one day we will regain our rightful place in Scotland. By the mid-seventeenth century it was already well known, judging from allusions to it in Gaelic poetry; in the songs of the Jacobite campaign of 1715 it had a prominent place: one of them begins with the words: 'This is the time when the Prophecy shall be fulfilled'. This messianic theme has always appeared to me to be an important element in the cultural life of Gaelic Scotland and psychologically important in the Jacobitism of the eighteenth century. Conventional historians disregard it.

Within the scope of this chapter I could only touch on a number of the more prominent aspects of Divination and the Seer. My bias overall would be to emphasise the aesthetic interest of stories and verses that are claimed to be the vehicles of divination. There are alternative ways of analysing the data, of course; but in this field, it seems to me, it is possible to see the creative imagination as strongly and as subtly at work as in other areas of what we call imaginative literature. Does this 'literature', however, have any other social function? Native ethnographers of the past have been at pains to point out that Gaelic 'Second Sight' is only a local variety of a global phenomenon. Nowadays, we tend more to stress our prerogative right to the 'gift'. That is to say, we use it positively in defining ourselves as Gaels over against the dominant cultures of Lowland Scotland and England. There is even a belief, presumably connected with the retreat of Gaelic into the North and West, that no one who is born far from the sea can possess Second Sight.

Finally, there is an interesting contrast between present and past accounts in what they imply is the relationship of precognition with the nature of fate. It is generally believed now that it is pointless for a seer to warn those who have been seen and recognised in a vision of disaster. (Portents and premonitions give room for manoeuvre.) The event has been preordained and fate cannot be averted. But it was not always so. Seers of the past had a duty to warn of approaching danger; evasive action was possible; fate was not fixed to that degree. A social anthropologist might see in this a reflection of the Gaelic sense of history. For many centuries Gaelic society has been subjected to a process of ethnocide. We once had some command over our destiny; now we have none. But whether this is what Gaelic seers, unconsciously it may be, have to tell us, I must leave to others to judge.

NOTES

1. This is the oldest form: Scots Gaelic *filidh*.

2. W. Matheson, 'The MacLeods of Lewis', *Trans.Gael.Soc.Inverness* 51 (19), 320–37, esp. 336.

3. *Miscellanea Scotica*: A Collection of Tracts relating to the History, Antiquities, Topography, and Literature of Scotland, III (Glasgow, 1820), 177–82.

4. *Ibid.*, 222–23.

5. Martin, like some other writers, is aware of this but does not consider that it 'communicates' the ability except for that occasion.

6. *Misc.Scot.* (note 3), 221.

7. *Ibid.*, 181–82.

8. *Carmina Gadelica* II, 158.

9. For this and other references to the use of the scapula, see *Trans.Gael.Soc.Glasgow* 5, 92–3.

10. *Misc.Scot.*, 190. In the same place he tells of a twelve-year-old girl haunted by her double.

11. *Gille-Martainn*, interestingly, is a bye-name in Gaelic for the fox, conventionally a trickster.

12. *Misc.Scot.* (note 3), 216–17. But another correspondent claims that only the 'vicious' have the sight: 'some say they get it by compact with the devil; some say by converse with these demons we call fairies'.

13. W. Matheson, 'The historical Coinneach Odhar and some prophecies attributed to him', *Trans.Gael.Soc.Inverness* 46 (19), 66–88. Cf. Alex. MacKenzie, *The Prophecies of the Brahan Seer* (Stirling, 1896).

2

Some Personal Experiences of the Second Sight

Eilidh Watt

'You know', said my niece, 'I was quite grown up before I realised that not everyone has a Presence with them to help and direct them. How do the others live?' Her observation, although at the time unexpected, did not really surprise me, for the spasmodic and involuntary ability to see events in the womb of time, generally those of a melancholy nature, has for generations been a characteristic of my father's family. The nature of this ability varies from person to person, but in whatever form it manifests itself, it is not in general considered a desirable faculty. It may indeed prove so harrowing that those who possess it may seek to have it removed. The recognised method is to have the leaves of the Bible riffled before the eyes of the sufferer while a minister prays for deliverance. I knew of a mother and son who were able both to see and hear. The mother was totally freed from these special powers, but the son was only partially freed and was still forced to hear. Were two 'forces' then involved, one in control of the seeing and one of the hearing? Since in general the possession of 'the two sights' is not considered to have a benign origin, the Power which the Bible symbolises was invoked. Here I may say that the Presence to which my niece referred was benign, making her aware of itself in time of need. To her mind, it was male, whilst I have 'female' visitors, who at times seem to be seeking information about me and depart when their curiosity is satisfied; I do not find them helpful.

Occasionally some who do not possess this faculty have sought to gain it. The generally accepted method is by placing the feet of the postulant on the feet of the seer when he is actually having a vision. The gift may also be transferred by hand-clasping, but it is essential that the seer wills the transfer. My father may have acquired his ability from his uncle, who once put his hand on him and drew him off the road to allow a phantom funeral procession to pass. They both watched the procession, recognised the mourners, heard women 'keening' for a drowned child. On the other hand my father may well have inherited the ability irrespective of this. What my father saw was never referred to in the presence of the

25

children for obvious reasons, and on one occasion only did I hear him make a prediction. He had been at a nephew's wedding on the mainland, and on his return we sat down to a meal and listened to his account of it. My mother was delighted that the groom's mother hoped to come and stay with us for a time when her son and his wife returned from their honeymoon, for she was my father's much loved sister. While my sister and I cleared the table, my parents still sat talking matters over, and I was returning for something when I was halted by my father lowering his voice and saying in a tone heavy with grief: 'You can make your plans, but Annie and I have met and parted for the last time on this side. She will die shortly. I saw the death veil shrouding her.' She died suddenly within three weeks.

Possibly from previous experience, he realised the significance of what he saw. The general belief is that if the veil is down at the knees, death is not imminent, but the nearer to the face it is, the nearer the person is to death. The person seen is not himself aware of any change in his appearance. In the Highlands a seeing such as this was not uncommon, and was interpreted as a sign of death. Naturally the seer made no reference to what he saw, but onlookers claimed that there was a kind of rigidity in his eyes at such moments.

The Church has no instruction regarding seeing, and one minister, a cousin who has experiences such as mine, regards it as of no more consequence than having a talent for music or handicraft. She makes no attempt to develop it or suppress it.

Recently with a friend I had occasion to go to a DIY shop run by a husband and wife. While the woman and my friend transacted some business in the office, I talked to the man, whom I had met briefly on previous occasions. I asked him how he had come to start a business in this rather remote part of the kingdom, for from his accent I concluded that he was not a native of the Island. He explained that although he was born in the Borders, his father was an Island man, and his mother, whose surname he gave, was also from the Highlands. I forget the surname, but it must have triggered some memory, for I said to him: 'So you must have the second sight'. For a moment he lidded his eyes and then looked up and admitted that he did. 'Can you detail a recent seeing for me?' I asked. He thought for a moment, and as if choosing a particular incident, said: 'One day I went into the office where the girl there was preparing to go for her lunch. I said to her: "When you are at a certain street junction be extra careful, for a green car will come round the corner travelling at excessive speed and will cause an accident". Amused, she went off, but when she neared the junction I had mentioned she slackened her pace, and observed the green car come as I had predicted. She was the main witness in the court case which followed.' Before I could question him further, we were joined by my friend, and I left.

The incident in itself is not important, but neither he nor I live in the world of important happenings. But the fact that he could see any happening in future time is of importance to our understanding of the universe and of our place in it. If we can see an event even minutes ahead of it taking place, then we can presume that events may be foreseen which will take place years and even centuries after the seeing. But since the world changes so rapidly, can we always understand what we see? From evidence given in law courts, it is not safe to assume that we can give an accurate description of what we saw. I think that reason sometimes tends to intervene and distort the 'seeing' in the light of our experience and to interpret it in that light.

That I myself should inherit this ability is not surprising, and I have seen the dead, spoken to them, and on occasion delivered messages to strangers who, unknown to me, had prayed for guidance or enlightenment. These incidents were sometimes amusing, sometimes embarrassing, and individually insignificant. However, I had one experience, to be described later, which so alarmed me that for years it was impossible to refer to it, and it affected my conception of the world. But the form of telepathy which I experience can have its lighter moments. For example, I had on one occasion on a chilly but sunny Sunday afternoon gone into the lower garden and searched in vain for signs of spring. Cold and disappointed, I returned to the warmth where my husband was reading the Sunday papers. Ignoring my complaints, he said: 'Well, I saw the Prattises going off in the car. Where do you think they were going?' Nettled by the question, I gave the most absurd answer which occurred to me: 'They have gone to the seaside to collect seaweed for your roses'. The absurdity lay in the fact that we were some distance from the sea, and that Mr Prattis was not exactly *persona grata* with my husband, since he was not above lopping off branches which shaded his garden seat. We read the Sunday papers.

On Monday, however, my husband came in from the garden and over tea asked what was clearly a momentous question: 'When were you last speaking to the Prattises?' 'Round about Christmas', I replied. 'I met them in town and they were very amusing about a disastrous autumn holiday in Mull.' 'Not since then?' 'No.' 'Well, there are two large plastic bags full of seaweed inside the side gate.' I could not account for them.

There were other incidents possibly of greater importance, although not necessarily so, when I acted in answer to other people's prayers; not infrequently these people were complete strangers to me. The recollection of one such incident is still vivid. A chain of events led me rather reluctantly to attend a union meeting one evening in a neighbouring town. I went in the company of a young male member of the staff and found the room filled almost to capacity, with only two vacant seats left after we had settled ourselves, one beside my companion and the other near the front. Just before the meeting started, two nuns appeared at the door scanning the room for vacant chairs. I am not a Roman Catholic and few in the preponderantly male audience were, but I asked my companion to move forward to the vacant chair and beckoned the nuns to the two seats next to me. There was no conversation between us, and the chairman opened the meeting at once. It was a lively one if not actually stormy, and I made more than one contribution. Finally the chairman indicated that there would be an interval to allow the wording of a motion and a chance for tempers to cool. At this juncture the nun nearer me spoke for the first time: 'Can you tell us how to teach drama in the infant room?'

It must by then have been clear to her that wherever my skills lay, they were not likely to be used in an infant room, and her voice was heavy with despair. Somewhat stung, I promptly answered: 'Yes, of course', and immediately embarked on a full and detailed account of method. I was only allowed a few sentences when she interrupted me and said to her companion: 'Write it down. This is the answer'. Without question the nun wrote at my rapid dictation. As happens on such occasions, the normal me stands aside and listens, sometimes with surprise or levity, or, as on this occasion, with a kind of impersonal admiration. This time all these feelings were fairly evenly balanced, for I had not entered an infant room from the time when I moved from it to a more senior class, and the teaching of drama in schools was still a new concept. The meeting resumed before I had finished and she had no time to thank me. I might well have forgotten the incident had she not turned to me as at the conclusion of the meeting and said: 'We have long prayed for guidance in this matter, and were were directed to come here tonight to have our prayers answered'. With that she turned and left.

Her attitude made such an impression on me that I wondered if I had read up the subject and forgotten about it. I went to the well-stocked library, generously financed by funds from the Carnegie Trust, to see if I could find anything, but there was nothing. On consideration, I thought that the ideas I had put forward were extremely practical, full of possibilities and full of fun. My own conclusions may be open to question, but the fact that the nuns had a deep conviction that their prayers had been answered is not. We can only believe what we ourselves experience, and may not necessarily draw the right conclusions, but for us they are right.

I may be directed to answer prayers at some inconvenience to myself. I may miss a bus and have to make a detour to meet the person involved. A chain of trivial events may lead me to a particular person. On occasion I become very restless and feel that there is somebody whom I must visit, even if I have not visited this person previously, and on the way make up what seem to me the feeblest of excuses for doing so. Rarely have the excuses been used, for I am greeted with the words: 'I thought you were never coming', or 'I have been asking God to send you'. When I arrive, my convenience is taken for granted, and I am there to nurse, fill in forms, or dissuade from suicide. I am left with the feeling that I am expendable. On the other hand I by nature am prepared to be expended in the interest of my fellows.

Sometimes I find myself speaking with a strange authority, as when a psychiatrist from an internationally known hospital, a stranger to me, ran up and asked permission to send a certain woman patient to a psychiatric hospital. I knew the woman and had visited her in hospital but was not related to her. I refused my consent, and explained that the mental confusion he claimed she was suffering from was temporary and would pass in a couple of days. I suggested that he consult the anaesthetist, for I knew she had undergone surgery, and find out if a drug had been administered which might cause hallucinations, and that he must see the patient again and assess her condition. He rang later to say that he had seen her and felt that she would soon be able to go home. A trivial incident, but I felt that I had spoken out of character in that I had no knowledge of the effects of drugs and do not usually question the findings of experts in their own field. I knew the woman had close, caring relatives who should have been consulted.

One may not always realise that a person one sees is dead. I recollect picking up the milk bottles from the doorstep one morning and remarking to my husband as I passed the open door of his sitting-room that our neighbours, a recently married couple, had returned from holiday. 'When did they get back?' he asked conversationally, and I replied: 'I don't know, but I saw Ronald walking down the drive as I picked up the milk.' Later in the forenoon my husband called me to the door where I found him with Ronald's works manager. They wanted to know when I had seen Ronald and I was reasonably sure of the exact time. 'Are you sure it was Ronald?' 'Yes, quite sure.' 'It is just that I have had a message', said the works manager, 'and I have to go down to Harrogate where Ronald died this morning. They were hoping to be back later today. You must have been mistaken.' 'Yes, I must', I admitted, for how could I explain that although Ronald's body remained at Harrogate, Ronald's other self had continued the journey and I had seen him quite unmistakably. In the light of other occasions when I saw dead people, I was interested to note that he wore the nylon shirt tucked into this flannels which was his normal wear; I judged that he had been formally dressed at Harrogate. The clothes which ghosts wear are of interest to me.

One forenoon about eighteen months after my husband had died after a prolonged fight against emphysema, I left the CAB office where I did voluntary work twice a week. It had been quite a busy session and I was glad to get into the spring sunshine. I decided to cross the Abbey churchyard and so avoid the town centre with its narrow crowded streets. I had just passed the Abbey when directly opposite at the futher end of the path I saw my husband approaching smoothly and rapidly. But he was visible only from the armpits down, as if I could see only what he could see of himself as he looked down. Although he was some little distance from me, I could see each detail clearly as if he were but a yard away. Whilst he appeared to walk, I had the impression that his feet did not actually touch the ground. He was dressed in a double-breasted suit long out of fashion, and was wearing equally unfashionable shoes in the style of about forty years ago. He seemed supremely happy, and I felt that he was reliving a period of his life when he had been very happy. I may add that I had never seen him in this area of the town, and his body, at his own wish, had been cremated.

As he seemed to approach me, I felt he would collide with me if I remained on the path. I stood aside, and at the same moment looked behind me in the hope that there might be someone else there whom I could question, but there was on one. When I looked back on the path there was no one, nothing. Though he seemed to be within a couple of yards from me, I felt that he was unaware of my presence. I experienced no fear, no chill, only a faint surprise as if I had seen a rose in bloom in winter. In life he was convinced that there was no existence after death.

On several earlier occasions I had the feeling that I looked briefly through the eyes of others, seeing what they saw; sometimes experienced pleasure, sometimes indignation, or sometimes a deep grief. On one such occasion I was crossing the street when the houses and people were briefly replaced by a very different scene. I saw a soaring headland, its black base washed by a restless sea but all lit by a cold sunshine. I felt that I was looking through the eyes of someone who knew that the familiar and loved scene would soon be hidden from him by death. I sensed that I had looked through the eyes of my uncle, a deeply religious man and a lay preacher of considerable standing. Since I believe there is a purpose in things, I wrote to him saying that I felt that the whole community valued his work. In reply I had a rather frigid note from his daughter, who thanked me and added that her father was in good health and had recently ventured out on a sunny day. A few days after this I had news of his death. By the time I had crossed the street on this occasion I realised that I could well have been killed had 'seeing' been more prolonged, and that in the modern world seers may be in physical danger.

But there are no words in any language I know which can give a realistic impression of the sense of evil which I once felt rayed its destructive force directly at me. The effect was so devastating that I can believe that if others experienced something similar they might not refer to it for fear of being considered mentally deranged, so not-of-the-earth was it. Only once have I heard anyone refer to such an experience. Henry James senior, the father of the novelist and of William James the philosopher, describes a personal happening in his book *Society: the Redeemed Form of Man*, published in Boston in 1879. It came to him at a time when he was sitting at home and at ease:

> One day towards the close of May, having eaten a comfortable dinner, I remained sitting at the table after the family had dispersed, idly gazing at the embers in the grate, thinking of nothing, and feeling only the exhilaration incident to a good digestion, when suddenly — in a lightning flash as it were — 'fear came upon me, and trembling, which made all my bones to shake'. To all appearance it was a perfectly insane and abject terror, without ostensible cause, and only to be accounted for, to my perplexed imagination, by some damnèd shape squatting invisible to me within the precincts of the room, and raying out from his fetid personality influences fatal to life. The thing had not lasted ten seconds before I felt myself a wreck, that is, reduced from a state of firm, vigorous, joyful manhood to one of almost helpless infancy. (pp. 44–5)

I went through an experience similar to this when I was an undergraduate in Glasgow. I had spent a pleasant time with friends, and in the early evening was returning to my lodgings by subway, a familiar journey. Travel conditions were easy and normal, and the compartment I travelled in had only two other occupants, a middle-aged, bowler-hatted man in the corner diagonally opposite me, and in the corner on my side a girl of about my own age. Suddenly I became aware of an invisible evil presence from which destructive rays seemed to emanate; although I could not locate its position it did not seem to be at ground level. I glanced at my travelling companions, who seemed undisturbed. I myself did not feel physically threatened, but my mind, or that other part of me which I have often been distinctly aware of as being other than my physical body, was being viciously attacked. I decided to leave the subway and walk the rest of the way. The sense of evil, of being under attack, diminished, but though I may have appeared normal, for days I felt as if a direct and murderous attack had been made on the essence of my being by a force completely alien, indescribably evil. It was a relief some ten years after the event to think that it was the same evil force that was dictating the extermination of the Jews to receptive ears. It seemed to me that for ten years or more all sources of Evil had been combining to overwhelm Good.

Does an outside force communicate with us? In the constitution of some of us is there a sort of 'receiver' which receives these messages, which may then be rejected or accepted according to the light of our own experience? Can there be free will if some of us are genetically conditioned to receive such messages? Many thinking people reject the idea that it is possible to see events yet to be enacted, on the grounds that it would destroy the belief in free will. That we may wish to think of ourselves as masters of our destinies may merely be a case of the wish being father to the thought. But seeing future events does not in itself deny us free will. Seers may see a man fall over a cliff, and fall over a cliff he will. We can see the act, but not the thinking which led him to the top of the cliff. Before the act he had the choice. Shakespeare had to resort to soliloquies to solve a similar problem of presentation.

I believe that I have a co-walker, and am sometimes of the opinion that there may be more than one, each possibly with different functions. One at least may have a brief existence apart from me. On one occasion, failing to fall asleep immediately on going to bed, I decided that in sleep I would visit my brother. In actual life the journey is somewhat involved and tedious. I fell asleep as soon as I had made the decision and slept dreamlessly until morning.

The following evening my brother's wife rang and asked after my health. On being reassured that I and immediate relatives were well, she said with more than a hint of exasperation in her voice: 'Well, your brother is very agitated and would not phone himself. He was convinced that you must have died. In the afternoon he returned from walking the dog and sat down to rest for a moment or two. Then you walked in. For a short time you talked, all quite normal even when you said you must go, bade him goodbye and went. I had been sitting outside in the sunshine, and when he joined me he asked if I had seen you. So real and normal it had been that it was difficult to convince him that it would have been impossible for anyone to enter the house without my seeing them. When I did convince him, he was sure you had died. I do wish that you would stop your ploys'. I accepted the rebuke, but found the time-lag of some sixteen hours interesting. I myself had no knowledge of the visit and gained no information. I had behaved completely in character.

I had another interesting experience when as a young adult I lived in my parents' home in a somewhat isolated part of the Island. There were few entertainments, and when the family doctor paid a visit the young man and I spent a pleasant afternoon together. Later in the day my mother suggested that I should go to enquire after an old man who had come to live with a married daughter and was believed to be in failing health. Dutifully, I went. I was welcomed by the middle-aged daughter, whom I knew slightly, and presently she said: 'I must take you to see father. He does love to have visitors, and the more so since he has been confined to bed'.

When we went into the bedroom, the daughter said cheerfully: 'Here's a visitor for you, father, but you don't know her'. 'Of course I know her', he retorted, 'she's the woman who was here with that young doctor.' From his exasperated tone it was clear that he did not like the young woman, and the daughter said apologetically: 'Father is somewhat confused today'. The old man said: 'Father is not confused today or any other day. I told you she kept coming between the doctor and the light and distracting him.' I sidled out. There was only one point clear to me, and that was that the old man could not possibly have known where the doctor had spent the couple of hours before his visit. What is still not clear is who it was that the old man saw. So widespread is the belief that we have a double that it is not uncommon for people to say: 'It must have been my double you saw' without examining what lies behind the saying.

Man's kinship with and power over animals is a difficult but interesting field of study. There are many incidents in this field which have baffled me. On one occasion a friend of my father visited our home. Both men were interested in cattle breeding in a small way and often compared results. Various bodies tried to foster interest in this subject by patronage at various cattle shows. Their overheard comments gave me food for thought, so I often followed them about the yard, never calling attention to myself. On this occasion they were discussing the visitor's exhibits at a local show, and one animal in particular. After a meditative silence, the man cast a wary eye in my direction before he made the riveting observation: 'Someone has put the evil eye on it'. My father expressed surprise, but not disbelief. He questioned the man about the symptoms and how he had treated the animal. 'I countered power with power', was the reply.

Later I understood that the method used was the common one: the silver coin in water fed by three burns, the midnight hour, the spoken charm. 'What words did you use?' my father asked. The answer was dramatic: 'Words which I will never again utter, though there should be neither horn nor hoof in my byre. In no conceivable circumstance would I repeat that operation. Oh yes, it was effective, but the cost was too high, too high'. Later I was to hear people wonder what had made him a changed man whom misfortune seemed to dog. It was not entirely that he had convinced himself he was *devotus*, doomed to destruction, and must pay the price and keep his side of the bargain. True, the animal might have recovered had it been left to itself. His own death was sudden and untimely. The Bible story of the Fall may support the belief that the price paid for knowledge and resulting brief power is too often a heavy one.

Animals are credited with the ability to see what the normal person does not. When I was a child we lived for a time beside an undertaker in a tiny village. I recollect standing at the door with my parents one day watching a horseman ride past. When he reached the undertaker's work place the horse refused to go on, in spite of the rider's efforts. My mother said in answer to a question from me: 'The horse is afraid, for he is seeing a spirit'. My father made no remark, but walked towards the horse and rider. I judge that he asked the rider to dismount, for this he did, and then my father took charge of the animal, putting an arm over its head and covering the horse's eyes with his hands. He then walked the horse, now quite sedate, beyond the workshop and duly delivered it to its rider. My father was said to be 'good with horses'. But of greater interest is the question of the horse's fear. Why should a horse find it unnatural to see a ghost?

Some years later we lived beside an old man long retired from work but with an excellent memory for incidents in an eventful life. As a shepherd he often drove flocks of sheep to the markets in Carlisle, involving him in a trek of many days. Man and animals required rest on the way, and there were farms which provided food and shelter. Even in old age he was a personable man and naturally made friends along the route. On one occasion he met a young man who had previously proved friendly and helpful, and now pointed out that instead of going to the usual farm and paying the dues, he would save money if he went to a spot which he would show him. It seemed eminently suitable, and the shepherd was grateful. By early evening the flock was resting; the shepherd had eaten and prepared for sleep by taking off his boots and putting his stockinged feet on the body of his old dog while he took the young bitch under his plaid where they would both be warm.

The tired flock showed no inclination to wander, and soon shepherd and dogs were asleep. However, the shepherd was awakened by the two dogs trembling violently and whimpering in low key as they strove to cower more closely to him. The man then heard the smack of blows, grunts and curses and occasionally women's cries. It was clear to him that the dogs saw something which terrified them, for their eyes were focused on the area from which the sounds came. He put on his boots, gathered the dogs to him and waited. After a time the sound of thudding blows ceased and there was a terrible silence. The sheep seemed unmoved throughout. By early morning he had his flock on the move. It was still early when he met the farmer whose fields he usually rented, and who was surprised to find him on his way so soon. The shepherd explained, and the farmer gave a brief and unflattering character sketch of the young man who had directed him to that spot. He knew, as everyone in that area knew, that the spot was haunted. Tinkers used to camp there, but no longer do, from the time that two tinkers fought to the death there.

There are a number of interesting points to be noted. The dogs were aware of the fight before the man, and were in a state of terror when he awoke. We can understand man's fear of the unnatural and unexplained, but did the dogs regard the incident in the same light? The sheep seemed unconcerned and were possibly unaware of what was going on. In the Highlands it is believed that certain animals only have the second sight. There is also the question of how often the incident was rehearsed? Clearly it is not a continuous performance, or man and dogs would have been aware of it when they reached the spot. It seems unlikely to be caused by energy from one of the participants, nor can one imagine all those involved being induced to re-enact the scene. And to what purpose? It is rather as if a 'recording' of the incident had taken place and that a disc jockey played it at unpredictable times. Are all sounds and actions recorded? Are they all played back?

I remember that a friend, the wife of a doctor, stayed once in a house where a woman had been murdered. The couple were incomers to the area and had been allocated the house in the hope of proving that it was not really haunted. The doctor and his wife and friends who visited them all heard a commotion in an upstairs bedroom, but the times of day when this occurred and the frequency were unpredictable and the pattern erratic. Another friend, a minister of the church, and his wife, who were home on leave from Africa, were walking across a stretch of moorland near the manse which they were occupying at the time when suddenly they heard what they took to be a clash of arms. The noise continued for some minutes, but they saw nothing out of the ordinary. When they mentioned the incident in the village in north-east Scotland near to the place, they were told that long ago a battle had been fought between rival clans, and that the sounds persist over the centuries and are heard periodically. The local people were only mildly interested.

Once when I was motoring in Fife with a friend we decided to stop and drink from our flasks of tea at the first attractive spot we found. There was one with groups of trees, two streams converging and an air of tranquillity which seemed admirably suited to our purpose, and leaving the car we made for the clearing. My friend was unpacking the basket when I cried out in a panic: 'I can't stay here! There have been blood sacrifices here!' and fled. In the car I asked her what the place was called. 'Shank of Navitie', ws the answer. From the name it may have had early Christian associations, but I am unable to account for my panic and for my declaration. I have been affected by other places but never to such a degree.

In the Highlands people are particularly interested in inherited characteristics, but one point has baffled us. Why are members of the same family so different? It seems that certain factors are dormant in some cases and very much in evidence in others. If it is believed that God the Creator is deliberately affecting changes, then there are no random happenings, but the purpose may not necessarily be seen by human beings. Perhaps the real point at issue is the nature of man. I have never been able to decide with what part of ourselves we feel emotions. Great grief, love, anger — any such emotion can affect the physical body but they do not have their seat in it. How and at what part is this other 'body' connected with the physical one? I tend to think of it as the flame at the candle wick, the burning coal.

3

The Saint as Seer: Adomnan's Account of Columba

John MacQueen

The image of Columba (c.521–597) as primarily a missionary saint is the creation of the Venerable Bede, who completed his *Historia Ecclesiastica* in 731, almost a hundred and fifty years after Columba's death. In Book III, chapter 4 he presents him as the apostle of the Northern Picts and the man who created in Iona a centre of missionary enterprise which eventually contributed a great deal to the Christianisation, not only of Scotland, but of much of northern and midland England as well. The earlier biography, written in or about 796 by Adomnan,[1] Columba's relative and eighth successor as abbot of Iona, gives a picture different in emphasis as well as historical detail, which in many ways also comes closer to the interests of the student of folklore. Chronological sequence is deliberately treated as of secondary importance; instead the biography is divided thematically into three books, the first of which deals with prophetic revelations granted by and to the saint, the second with miracles of power, 'often accompanied by prophetic foreknowledge'; the third is concerned with angelic apparitions 'that were revealed to others in relation to the blessed man, or to him in relation to others, and concerning those that were made visible to both, though in unequal measure (that is, to him directly and more fully, and to others indirectly and only in part, that is to say, from without and by stealth), but in the same visions, either of angels, or of heavenly light'.[2] Columba, in other words, is treated primarily as a seer, whose abilities reached across time and space, and were capable of perceiving spiritual as well as physical entities.

Columba was able to see things concealed from others in a number of ways, several among them illustrated by chapter 3 of Book I, which deals with events during a visit which he made to the famous Irish monastery of Clonmacnoise in Co. Offaly. He perceived first of all that a boy, Ernene, Crasen's son, was standing behind his back touching the hem of his cloak. Secondly he foresaw that although the boy was despised in the monastery, he was destined to become a man particularly distinguished in the church for his eloquence. He also foresaw the dispute about the

37

time of the Easter festival which later became of such importance to the Celtic church generally. Finally he noticed that certain places about the monastery were frequented by angels whose presence had not hitherto been suspected by the brethren.

Only two of these four events involve prophecy in the usual sense of the word, and one even of these was probably interpolated by Adomnan, who was himself much involved with the Easter question.[3] Columba died in 597. In 632 many of the southern Irish churches adopted the Roman method of calculating the date of Easter; Adomnan himself persuaded the northerners to follow suit just before the end of the century, but even so was unable to win the allegiance of his own community in Iona. He probably left it as a consequence. It was obviously a matter of some distress to him that his great and venerated predecessor had followed a system different from his own, and the passage in chapter 3 probably forms part of his campaign to win monks of the Columban family to the true belief. To have said that Columba followed the Roman rule would have strained anyone's credulity, but to make him prophesy with approval its adoption was potentially an effective weapon, one in actuality so far as the northern Irish churches were concerned. The prophecy itself, however, has little or nothing to do with folklore studies.

The second prophecy, that of the future eminence of an apparently undistinguished child, comes closer to the norm.[4] The name Ernene, Crasen's son, may not convey much to the modern reader; the meaning is 'little iron man', and in its hypocoristic form with the affectionate prefixed *mo*, 'my', it is possible that it may be preserved in Kilmarnock, 'church of my Ernoc', in the modern Ayrshire,[5] and that some further tradition about him lingers in the figure of Mernoc, the procurator of the *terra repromissionis sanctorum*, the 'land of the second promise made to the saints', in the *Voyage of St Brendan*.[6]

Prophecy is absent from the other two. In the first Columba perceives the physical presence of the boy when there is no apparent way in which he could have gained such knowledge. Perceptions of this kind, when direct view is blocked, or the object is at an apparently impossible distance, are recurrent in the *Life*. In Book I, chapter 41, for instance, Columba calls two of the brethren to him, and says: 'Now cross the strait to the island of Mull, and look for the thief Erc, in the little plains beside the sea. He came last night secretly, alone, from the isle of Coll, and he is trying to conceal himself during the day among sand-hills, under his boat which he has covered with grass; so that by night he may sail across to the small island where the sea-calves that pertain to us breed and are bred; in order that the greedy robber may fill his boat with those that he thievishly kills, and make his way back to his dwelling'.

The rather stilted Latin of the passage cannot disguise the detailed physical reality of the saint's vision — the machair with its sand-hills, the inverted boat covered with grass, the thief himself crouched below, the little breeding island for the seals, which are regarded as a kind of monastic cattle. No element of prophecy is present. Columba sees the man's intentions, and frustrates them by having him arrested and sent home with a gift of mutton instead of seal-flesh. Erc himself obviously lives on the borderline of starvation. An element of saintly compassion comes into the story and its immediate sequel, the account of the gift of food sent by the saint, which arrived too late, and was used instead at Erc's funeral.

This element of compassion recurs in chapter 48, which also involves a certain measure of prophecy, although in human terms the importance of the event prophesied is negligible. The saint tells one of the brethren: 'On the third day from this that dawns, you must watch in the western part of this island, sitting above the sea-shore; for after the ninth hour of the day a guest will arrive from the northern region of Ireland, very tired and weary, a crane that has been tossed by winds through long circuits of the air. And with its strength almost exhausted it will fall near you and lie upon the shore. You will take heed to lift it tenderly, and carry it to the house near by; and having taken it in as a guest there for the space of three days and nights, you will wait upon it and feed it with anxious care. And afterwards, at the end of the three days, revived and not wishing to be longer in pilgrimage with us, it will return with fully recovered strength to the sweet district of Ireland from which at first it came. I commend it to you thus earnestly, for this reason, that it comes from the district of our fathers'.

The physical clarity of the vision is again noticeable, as it also is in the conclusion of the story: 'This, precisely as the saint foretold, the event also proved to be true. After being a guest for three days, it [the crane] first rose from the ground in the presence of its host that had cared for it, and flew to a height; and then, after studying the way for a while in the air, crossed the expanse of ocean, and in calm weather took its way back to Ireland, in a straight line of flight'.

A computer-like speed and accuracy of short-range perception is to be found in chapter 23, the story of the vowel I. Baithene, one of the senior brethren, later Columba's successor, had completed the copying of a manuscript psalter, and proposed that someone else should check it for errors of transcription. Columba commented: 'Why do you impose this trouble upon us without cause? Since in this psalter of yours, of which you speak, neither will one letter be found to be superfluous, nor another to have been left out; except a vowel I, which alone is missing'. Needless to say, when the manuscript was checked, Columba's words were found to have been true.

This might, I suppose, be interpreted in either of two ways, Columba might have miraculously scanned the manuscript and seen that one letter was missing. Alternatively, he might have prophetically foreseen the result of the check. Adomnan's narrative certainly encourages the former interpretation.

The miracle of the letter did not involve sight at any notable remove; in the others quoted, the maximum distance involved was of the order of two miles. Perhaps, however, one should take into account such features as the saint's knowledge that Erc had come from Coll, twenty-five miles away, or that the crane had flown the hundred miles that separate Iona from Columba's ancestral home in Donegal. Some of the miracles involve more substantial distances still; I.29 may be quoted in which he sees from Iona on a very cold winter day that Laisran, Feradach's son, the future third abbot of Iona, is overworking the monks who are engaged in building the new monastery at Durrow in Co. Offaly, another Columban foundation, some two hundred and twenty-five miles to the south. Adomnan indicates that Columba was able to communicate his distress across such a distance; at the very moment when the comment was made, Laisran 'being in some way impelled, and as if kindled with an inward fire, ordered that the monks should cease work; that some consolation of food should be prepared; and that they should not only take leisure on that day, but also rest on the remaining days of rough weather'. The saint of course heard these instructions in the spirit and was delighted. He combined, in other words, the power of seeing with that of hearing at a distance.

In this kind his most spectacular feats were to see the destruction of a city in Italy (I.28), which Notker Balbulus (c.840–912) saw as a reference to the destruction of Citta Nuova in Istria, and to supervise the voyages made by Cormac, grandson of Lethan, into remote northern waters (I.6, II.42).

Columba foresaw that the exhausted crane would arrive in three days' time, and depart three days later still. Some other miracles involving foreknowledge are on the same miniature timescale. I.4 contains the prophecy, made on a stormy day, that Cainnech would arrive during the evening. The brethren discount the idea, but the saintliness of Cainnech is more powerful than the storm, and he duly arrives at the time stated. In I.16 Columba prophesies on a Saturday that a certain young man will die on the following Friday, and be buried in Iona in a week's time. Some of his forecasts, however, are more long-range. No precise date, for instance, is given for the future eminence of Ernene, Crasen's son, already mentioned, but Adomnan says that Ernene himself mentioned the prophecy in conversation with Segene, fifth abbot of Iona, who died in 652. Failbe, the eighth abbot, who died in 679, was also present, so it is perhaps fair to assume that the conversation took place during Segene's last days, fifty years or so after the death of Columba, and that the distinction of Ernene was by then well established. Adomnan must have believed that to make the prophecy Columba looked ten or fifteen years, perhaps longer, into the future.

An even longer prospect is presupposed by some of the stories, which also on occasion involve events of greater general significance than any yet mentioned. In 575 Columba attended the Convention of Druim Ceit (Mullagh in Co. Derry), where Aed, the high-king of Ireland, met Aedan, king of the Irish and Scottish DalRiada, to discuss their differing responsibilities and the tributes due to both from the Irish territory.[7] At this time Aed held Scandlan, Colman's son, a member of the royal kinship-group in Osraige (Ossory), as prisoner or hostage. Columba visited the young man in prison, and comforted him with the prophecy that he would outlive Aed, and return from exile to reign as king of his own people for thirty years. Another period of exile would follow, from which he would return to reign for three short seasons.

The sequel is best given in Adomnan's own words: 'All these things were entirely fulfilled according to the saint's prophecy. For after thirty years he [Scandlan] was driven from the kingdom, and was in exile for some period of time; but afterwards, recalled by the people, he reigned, not for three years, as he supposed he should, but for three months, immediately after which he died'.

Scandlan died as king of Osraige in 644, sixty-nine years after the delivery of the prophecy. Here we have one of several instances of Columba's reluctance to give anyone an unambiguous idea of the time of his death.

The succession to the DalRiadic kingship held by Aedan is the focus of another group of two tales (I.8 and 9), which involve prophecy, and also Columba's ability to perceive events as they happened at a distance. The battle with the Miathi in 583 or 584 was one of the crucial events of Aedan's long reign. It probably took place somewhere in the vicinity of Stirling or Falkirk, a hundred and fifteen miles distant from Iona. Aedan was the victor, but at a heavy cost, which included the lives of two of his three elder sons. The third, Domingart, was killed later, probably at the battle of Degsastan in 603. In 609 Aedan died, perhaps in religion, having the previous year been succeeded by Eochaid Buide, one of his younger sons.

In I.9 Columba informs Aedan that the line of succession will run through Eochaid Buide and his sons, as it did until 636, the year of the battle of Mag Rath, Moira in Co. Down, where Domnall Brecc, son of Eochaid Buide, together with his Irish allies was defeated by Domnall son of Aed, the Irish high-king.[8] The prophecy was made before the battle with the Miathi, and so involves a period of some fifty-five years.

Characteristically, the stories are not told in chronological order. I.8 tells how Columba summoned the brethren to pray for Aedan because the battle was just commencing, and how afterwards he went out, looked at the sky, and announced the king's victory, together with the casualties, which totalled three hundred and three. I.9 relates the king's question about the succession, and his assumption that one of his three elder sons would become king.[9] Columba answers that all three will predecease him, and Adomnan adds that two died during the battle with the Miathi already mentioned. Columba told Aedan that the son who was in fact to succeed would run to his knee when he was summoned with the other younger children, and this Eochaid Buide in fact did. The election is confirmed when he is kissed and blessed by the saint, but Columba had been dead for more than a decade when Eochaid actually came to the throne.

It should be added that in III.5 Adomnan quotes the report given by his predecessor, abbot Cumméne, of a warning made by Columba to Aedan that his descendants would lose their position if ever they 'did evil' to the *cenél Conaill*, the kindred to which the saint himself as well as the Irish high-kings belonged. Domnall Brecc forgot the prophecy when he fought at Mag Rath.

It is worth noting that in the instances quoted Columba's powers are presented as limited. He knows that a battle is taking place, but only knows the victor after the event; he knows that one of the younger sons will succeed, but knows the individual only after a particular act has been performed. He knows the consequences of a particular course of action by Aedan's descendants, but not apparently when or by whom it will be undertaken. A similar element enters many of the other instances of unusual perception on the part of the saint. He knows that someone remarkable is standing behind him as soon as Ernene, Crasen's son, touches the hem of his garment;[10] the specific ability, eloquence, involved, he does not know until he has examined the boy's tongue. (Parenthetically, it should be said that he had some idea; otherwise why should he have examined the tongue rather than any other significant part of the boy's body?) He does not know the precise duration of Scandlan's second reign, but he is aware that the number three is a significant element for the period. Scandlan assumes a three-year duration, but it turns out in fact to be three months.[11] In I.35 he tells Colcu, Cellach's son, that demons are dragging to hell one grasping leader from the chief men of his district, but does not name the man. 'When he heard this,

Colcu wrote down the date and the hour on a tablet. And returning to his country after some months, he learned by questioning, from people of the district, that Gallan, Fachtne's son, had died in the same hour in which the blessed man had told him of the seizure by demons.'

Colcu came from north-east Ireland, and the reference is to a district there, so here again we have an instance of Columba's power of seeing at a distance. Colcu might have asked the name of the man carried off, but abstained. We are thus left in some doubt as to whether it was believed that Columba knew his identity, but may perhaps assume that as the region of Ireland involved was distant from Columba's own, he did not; that he perceived the incident, but did not know the identity of the protagonist.

In one instance (I.47) Adomnan leads us to believe that the saint deliberately concealed the extent of his knowledge so that he might minimise the suspense and apprehension of the victim of his foresight. Gore, another son apparently of king Aedan, was the strongest man of his time, and asked the saint how he should die. The saint gave him a deliberately ambiguous answer: ' "You will die neither in battle, nor in the sea. A companion of your journey, from whom you suspect nothing, will be the cause of your death." "Perhaps", said Gore, "one of the friends that accompany me may have it in mind to kill me; or my wife, to contrive my death by magic art, for love of a younger man." The saint said: "It will not happen so". "Why", said Gore, "will you not tell me now about my slayer?" The saint replied: "I will not disclose anything to you more plainly now, about that baneful companion of yours, lest you be too greatly troubled by frequent remembrance of what you know, before the day comes on which you will learn the truth of this matter".'

'Why linger over words? After some years had passed, it chanced one day that the same Gore was sitting under a ship, and with his own knife was scraping the bark from a spear-shaft. Then he heard some men nearby fighting among themselves, and he rose quickly, to part the fighters; and his knee, striking against that knife, which in the sudden movement he had carelessly dropped on the ground, was severely wounded. And by this companion's doing, the cause of his death arose. Directly, with consternation of mind, he remembered that it was in accordance with the prophecy of the holy man. And after some months, oppressed by this evil, he died.'

Two factors are important here. One is that Gore asked the saint directly about the manner of his death, possibly in the expectation of hearing that it would take place in the course of some heroic exploit by land or sea. His question, in other words, contained some element of personal vanity, as did his reaction to Columba's answer, in which he sees himself as the central figure in a tragic romance. For such a man the circumstances of the actual death to which he was destined would be humiliating. The saint used terms which would preserve Gore's harmless illusions until the last moment.

Gore secondly was a layman, and so unfitted to have direct knowledge of a matter so closely involved with his salvation or damnation as death. For clerics it was different; Columba more than once[12] told men in holy orders the precise moment of their decease, which for them, he knew, would be the moment of rebirth to eternal life. He also knew the hour of his own departure; his fervent appeals had persuaded the Lord to grant that it would come when he had completed thirty years of pilgrimage on Iona, but the united prayers of the churches delayed the consummation for another four.[13] The arrival of the actual moment was heralded by an angel, invisible to everyone but the saint. Such conditions were appropriate only to sanctity, and might not be extended to a layman, however conspicuous his physical strength had made him. The ambiguity of this prophecy, that is to say, is governed, not by any failure of knowledge on the part of the saint, but by his perception of what was appropriate to the occasion and to the person involved. Gore could not escape the final humiliation, but at least he did not spend his last years in useless attempts to avoid the destiny which he found so unaccommodating to his ambitions.

Adomnan does not regard such powers of perception as in any way unique to Columba; he had them to an uncommon degree, but to some extent they might be shared by anyone whose way of life might be regarded as holy. A minor example of this has already been given in the story of Laisran and his overworked monks at Durrow, although here it is not clear that Laisren was fully aware of what was happening. A better instance is provided in II.13, the story of a stormy voyage made by the saint: 'Also at another time, when a very fierce and dangerous storm was blowing, and his companions importuned the saint to pray to the Lord for them, he gave them this answer, and said: "On this day it is not for me to pray for you in this danger that you are in; it is for the holy man, the abbot Cainnech".'

'I have marvellous things to tell. In the same hour, Saint Cainnech, being in his own monastery, which is in Latin called "field of the cow", and in Irish Ached-bou, by revelation of the Holy Spirit heard in the inner ear of his heart those words of Saint Columba. And since it chanced that he had begun after the ninth hour to break the holy bread in the refectory, he suddenly abandoned the small table, and with one shoe on his foot, and the other left behind through the excess of his haste, he went hurriedly to the church, with these words: "We cannot have dinner at this time, when Saint Columba's ship is in danger on the sea. For at this moment he repeatedly calls upon the name of this Cainnech, to pray to Christ for him, and his companions in peril". After saying these words he entered the oratory, bowed his knees, and prayed for a little while. The Lord heard his prayer, and at once the storm ceased, and the sea became perfectly calm'.

The detail here is again vivid. Cainnech is just sitting down to dinner in the refectory of his monastery at Aghaboe, co. Laois, when he hears the words of Columba and sees the plight of his company some two-hundred-and-fifty miles away. So great is his haste that one of his shoes falls off as he rushes to the church. His prayers are effective in stilling the distant storm. Columba, incidentally, from the ship perceives that Cainnech has run to the church wearing only one shoe.[14]

In I.3 Columba indicates to the brethren at Clonmacnoise, co. Offaly, that angels frequented certain parts of the monastic enclosure. No one else was able to see them. In the same way only he was able to see the company of angels who came from the east across Mull towards Iona to bring his soul to heaven when he had completed thirty years on the island. On this occasion the united prayers of the churches caused them to halt on a rock on the far side of the strait which separates the two islands, but again, four years later,[15] only Columba saw the angel who brought the final summons: 'Then after a few days had passed, while the rites of the Mass were being celebrated on a Lord's-day according to the custom, the venerable man lifted up his eyes, and suddenly his face was seen to flush with a ruddy glow; as it is written, "The countenance glows when the heart is glad"; and in fact at the same moment he alone saw an angel of the Lord hovering above, within the walls of the oratory itself; and because the calm and lovely sight of holy angels fills the hearts of the elect with joy and exultation, this was the cause of the sudden gladness that filled the blessed man.'

'When those who were present there asked about this, the cause of the gladness inspired in him, the saint, gazing upward, gave them this reply: "Wonderful and incomparable is the fineness of angelic nature! See, an angel of the Lord, sent to recover a deposit dear to God, looking down upon us within the church and blessing us, has returned through the roof-courses of the church, leaving no trace of that departure" '.

Columba also was empowered to command angels to perform tasks while themselves remaining invisible to others. The best instance is to be found in III.15, the chapter-heading of which reads 'Concerning an angel of the Lord, who came very quickly and opportunely to the rescue of a brother as he fell from the top of the round monastic house in the plain of the oakwood'. This is another reference to the building of the monastery at Durrow in co. Offaly. From Iona Columba saw a monk slip as he worked on the pinnacle of the roof of the highest part of the structure. At once he dispatched an angel, who was standing by, invisible to others, and who was able to break the man's fall before he touched the ground: 'he that fell was unable to feel any fracture or injury'. The comment made by Columba is more than apposite: 'Exceedingly marvellous and almost beyond description is the swiftness of angels' flight, equal as I think to the speed of lightning'.

Relations between the angelic orders and Columba might sometimes be strained, as the story (III.5) of the ordination of Aedan as king illustrates. Columba loved Iogenan[16] more than his brother Aedan, and was unwilling to act when an angel appeared to him by night in the island of Hinba (perhaps Jura), and presented him with a glass book[17] of the ordination of kings, which included the name of Aedan. As a consequence the angel struck him with a scourge, 'the livid scar from which remained on his side all the days of his life'. Despite the wound, the saint remained obstinate for two more nights, but eventually capitulated, and went to Iona, where he performed the ceremony and made a prophecy about Aedan's sons, grandsons and great-grandsons. This may have included the prophecy (I.9) about the deaths of Aedan's three elder sons and the succession of Eochaid Buide, but one MS inserts the prophecy already mentioned concerning relations between Aedan's kindred and the *cenél Conaill*, a prophecy given on the authority of Cumméne the White, seventh abbot of Iona from 657 until his death in 669. Cumméne wrote a book on the miraculous powers of Columba, which apart from this brief extract does not appear to have survived.[18] It is nevertheless possible and even likely that Adomnan's book is primarily a revision and expansion of this.

As several stories might illustrate, Columba was also capable of perceiving the activities of demons. The most notable instance is III.8, where in a remote part of his island he finds himself under attack from a foul and very black array of demons, armed with iron spits. The battle lasts most of the day, with Columba employing the Pauline whole armour of God in his defence; it is decided only when a band of angels comes to his support, and expels the demons to the west. They withdraw to Tiree, where they institute a plague, from which many of the religious communities on the island suffer grievously. The saint's exertions, however, ensure that Iona itself remains unaffected, as does one Tiree community, that governed by the Baithene already mentioned, Columba's kinsman and eventual successor, whose virtuous practices limited losses to a single monk.

One lesser encounter with a demon (II.16) is noteworthy. Colman, descendant of Briun, asked the saint to bless a vessel full of new milk which he was carrying on his back. When Columba obliged, the vessel 'was at once violently shaken. The fastening-peg of the lid was thrust back through its two holes, and thrown far off; the lid fell to the ground; the greater part of the milk was spilt upon the earth. The boy put down the vessel on its base, upon the ground, with the little that remained of the milk. He bowed his knees in supplication. The saint said to him: "Rise, Colman. You have been careless in your work today. Before the milk was poured in, you did not, by imprinting the sign of the Lord's cross, expel a demon that lurked in the bottom of the empty vessel. Now, unable to endure the power of that sign, by his trembling he has shaken the whole vessel, and has spilt the milk in his sudden flight. Bring hither therefore the vessel, nearer to me, so that I may bless it".'

'When this was done, the half-empty vessel that the saint had blessed was found in the same moment to have been divinely filled again; and the little that had remained before in the bottom of the vessel had, under the blessing of his holy hand, instantly swelled up to the brim'.

Demons, it will be noted, participate more than angels in the physical. An angel passed through the roof-courses of the church, leaving no trace, but the demon could escape from the saint's blessing only by unfastening the lid and spilling the milk. The saint too was able to see that Colman had previously failed in his duty — he had not blessed the vessel before filling it with milk, and thus had not disturbed the demon occupant.

Adomnan makes several comments on the nature of the powers which Columba possessed, sometimes placing them in the mouth of the saint himself. In I.1, for instance, he comments: 'So too, as this holy man of the Lord, Columba, himself admitted to a few brothers who once questioned him closely about this very thing, in some speculations[19] made with divine favour the scope of his mind was miraculously enlarged, and he saw plainly, and contemplated, even the whole world as it were caught up in one ray of the sun'. In I.43 the same words are repeated in answer to the questions of Lugbe mocu-Blai: 'There are some, although few indeed, on whom divine favour has bestowed the gift of contemplating, clearly and very distinctly, with scope of mind miraculously enlarged, in one and the same moment, as though under one ray of the sun, even the whole circle of the whole earth, with the ocean and sky about it'. To a degree these words are a reminiscence of a passage (cap. XXXV: *De mundo ante eius oculos collecto et anima Germani Capuanae civitatis episcopo*) in the second *Dialogue*[20] of Columba's contemporary, Pope Gregory the Great (c.540–604), written in 593/4. An echo will also be found in the fourth *Dialogue*.[21] The reference in both is to an experience of the great St Benedict of Nursia (c.480–c.550), 'the patriarch of Western monasticism', to whom a vision of celestial light was granted, by means of which he saw the entire creation brought before his eyes, as it were in one ray of the sun. As part of this he perceived that the soul of bishop Germanus of Capua was at that very moment being carried to heaven by a fiery globe of angels. Benedict, it should be noted, saw the fiery globe by virtue of the celestial light, the origin of which lay elsewhere and higher. There is nevertheless a clear kinship between the divine light and that which characterises the angelic orders, a kinship based on the mysticism of light found in St Augustine.[22]

Columba, like Benedict, experienced supernatural light, which sometimes was also seen by others; sometimes too it was accompanied by the apparition of angels. St Brendan of Birr in co. Offaly saw him, for instance, preceded by a pillar of fire and accompanied by angels (III.3). In III.18 the Holy Spirit is poured out on Columba 'for the space of three days, so that for three days and as many nights, remaining within a house barred, and filled with heavenly light, he allowed no one to go to him, and he neither ate nor drank. From that house beams of immeasurable brightness were visible in the night, escaping through chinks of the door-leaves, and through the key-holes. And spiritual songs, unheard before, were heard being sung by him. Moreover, as he afterwards admitted in the presence of a very few men, he saw, openly revealed, many of the secret things that have been hidden since the world began. Also everything that in the sacred scriptures is dark and most difficult became plain, and was shown more clearly than the day to the eyes of his purest heart. And he lamented that his foster-son Baithene was not there, who, if he had chanced to be present during those three days, would have written down from the mouth of the blessed man very many mysteries, both of past ages and of ages still to come, mysteries unknown to other men; and also a number of interpretations of the sacred books. But Baithene was detained in the island of Ege by contrary winds, and was unable to be present until those three days and nights of the incomparable and glorious visitation had come to an end'.

Apart from Columba, Baithene, his successor, was the only brother whose holiness was great enough to allow him to endure the light. The expression given to Columba's inspiration was oral, and could only have been recorded if someone else had been present to record what he said during his illumination.

The visitation took place on Hinba (Jura), where also an angel showed him the glass book of the ordination of kings. Adomnan may well have regarded supernatural light and angelic visitations as the source of Columba's powers. He makes it plain that Columba gained knowledge of past and future from the light, and the prophecies which deal with royal succession could have been based on the glass book.

To a degree this is confirmed by the casual reply which in I.18

Columba gives, when a monk ordered to sail to Ireland complains that one of his crew has not reported for duty: 'The sailor who, you tell me, has not yet come forward, I cannot at present find'. There is no suggestion that the saint has ordered any search to be made by others, or himself undertaken any bodily exertion. Rather he has dispatched his spirit to make an instant survey of the island, the negative result of which he gives almost immediately. His spirit, in other words, is not confined to his body, but is capable of independent travel and of making physical observations. I.37, 'Concerning a certain relief by the holy man's spirit, sent to labouring monks upon the way', is a further striking example. Harvest workers returning wearily in the evening from the little western plain of the island always felt a certain refreshment at a place called Cul Eilne, which marked the halfway stage on their walk back to the monastery. Baithene, who was in charge of the party, and whose holiness and spiritual insight have already been emphasised, gave this explanation: 'You know that our senior, Columba, thinks of us with solicitude, and, mindful of our labour, is much distressed when we are late in reaching him. And for the reason that he does not come in the body to meet us, his spirit meets us as we walk, and in this fashion refeshes and gladdens us'. One receives the impression that Columba's 'spirit' maintained a constant patrol round Iona, and indeed the western approaches generally, and that this was held to explain many of his feats as seer and miracle-worker. Late Latin *spiritus*, it should be noted, may be translated 'spiritual being' as well as 'soul'; Adomnan's words, that is to say, leave open the possibility that the spirit was in fact an angel. Whatever its nature, it was capable of seeing and influencing distant events, future as well as present.

I hope it will now be clear that the oldest complete surviving record of Columba is not biography or history in any modern sense; rather it is a collection of material of folk and anthropological interest, the marked tendency of which is to emphasise a late seventh-century belief in the range and power of the saint's clairvoyant and prophetic abilities. Such beliefs tend to be associated with particular persons and places, to take the form of local legends or the like, and this too has an obvious relevance for Adomnan's three books. The relationship between such material and the historical figure of Columba must, I suggest, for ever remain obscure.

NOTES

1. A. O. and M. O. Anderson (eds.), *Adomnan's Life of Columba* (London and Edinburgh, 1961). Hereafter *Columba*.

2. *Columba*, 325, 465.

3. The best account is still 'Excursus on the Paschal Controversy and Tonsure', C. Plummer, *Baedae Opera Historica* (2 vols., Oxford, 1896), ii, 348–54.

4. Cf., for instance, the undistinguished childhood of Beowulf (*Beowulf*, 2183–9) which forms part of what Friedrich Panzer called the Bear's Son Tale (*Studien zur germanischen Sagengeschichte. I. Beowulf* [München, 1910]).

5. W. J. Watson, *History of the Celtic Place Names of Scotland* (Edinburgh and London, 1926), 187–8, 291.

6. C. Selmar (ed.), *Navigatio Sancti Brendani Abbatis* (Notre Dame, 1959); translation in J. F. Webb, *Lives of the Saints* (Harmondsworth, 1965), 33–68.

7. See especially F. J. Byrne, *Irish Kings and High-Kings* (London, 1973), 110–11; M. O. Anderson, *Kings and Kingship in Early Scotland* (Edinburgh and London, 1980), 146–9.

8. Byrne, *op. cit.*, 112–4; M. O. Anderson, *op. cit.*, 152, 156–7.

9. On the Gaelic law of succession to the kingship, see Byrne, *op. cit.*, 35–9, 122–3.

10. There is a reference here to Luke 8:43–8, the miraculous healing of the woman with the issue of blood.

11. Three is itself a supernatural number, with associations appropriate to prophecy.

12. See, *e.g.*, I.31, 32. Columba sometimes prophesied to reprobates the date of their death, a prophecy generally mocked or ignored. See I.27, II.23.

13. It is perhaps worth noting that Christ was in his thirty-fourth year at the time of the Crucifixion. In the early French *Vie de Saint Alexis*, the saint devotes a total of thirty-four years to his austerities. See J. MacQueen, *Numerology* (Edinburgh, 1985), 71–2.

14. The same story will be found in *Vita S. Cainnechi*, 54 (W. W. Heist, ed., *Vitae Sanctorum Hiberniae*, [Bruxelles, 1965], 196).

15. See above, note 13.

16. By the Gaelic law of royal succession (above, note 9) Iogenan's claim was as strong as Aedan's.

17. Byrne, *op. cit.*, 255, suggests that this was 'a book with an enamelled cover rather than "a book of glass"'. The Latin is *liber vitreus*.

18. See *Columba*, 12–17.

19. The word 'speculations' has misleading connotations as a translation of Latin *speculationibus*. This is indicated by such texts as Boethius, *De Consolatione Philosophiae*, V.ii: *Humanas vero animas liberiores quidem esse necesse est cum se in mentis divinae speculatione conservant, minus vero cum dilabuntur ad corpora, minusque etiam, cum terrenis artubus colligantur*, 'Human souls necessarily have more freedom when they preserve themselves in contemplation (*speculatione*) of the divine mind, less so when they are dispersed towards bodies, even less when they are tethered to earthly limbs'. The connotations of the word are Neoplatonic; it derives from the same root as *speculum*, 'mirror' and presupposes the system of emanations and reflections which make up the Neoplatonic cosmos. 'Mind emanates from the Supreme God and Soul from Mind, and Mind, indeed, forms and suffuses all below with life, and . . . this is the one splendour lighting up everything and visible in all, like a countenance reflected in many mirrors arranged in a row' (Macrobius, *Commentary on the Dream of Scipio*, trs., W. H. Stahl, New York and London, 1952, 145): 'It is illumination by Mind that makes Soul intelligent, and Mind is compared to the sun, some of whose light is retained by the soul. Since in Plotinus, Mind and the (Platonic) Forms are identical, this is equivalent to saying that the soul is illuminated or irradiated (the phrase is that of Plotinus) by the Forms' (David Knowles, *The Evolution of Medieval Thought* [London, 1962], 44).

20. U. Morricca (ed.), *Gregorii Magni Dialogi* (Roma: Istituto Storico Italiano, 1924), 129 (II.35).

21. Moricca, *op. cit.*, 240 (IV.8)

22. In Augustine, 'the Plotinian Mind is replaced by the divine Word, and the human soul is the recipient of Its illumination; Its light irradiates into the soul the immaterial intelligible objects — forms, ideas, reasons, rules — and illuminates them for its perception' (Knowles, *loc. cit.*).

4

Prophecy in Middle Welsh Tradition

Juliette Wood

In Shakespeare's play *Richard II*, a Welsh captain reports that the Welsh troops have dispersed because of unfavorable portents:

> The bay-trees in our country are all withered
> And meteors fright the fixed stars of heaven
> The pale-faced moon looks bloody on the earth
> And lean-looked prophets whisper fearful change. . .
> These signs forerun the death or fall of kings.[1]

The incident reflects a widely held belief that the Welsh were easily swayed by prophetic utterances. Ralph of Higden also reports that the Welsh listen to prophecies, specifically that '. . . the prophecy of Merlin and his witchcraft was wont to beguile them and to move them into battle . . .'[2] As late as the reign of Henry VIII, the English authorities were still worried about the possible effects of this kind of tradition on their Welsh subjects. A Tudor spy reported that they spent their Sundays listening to the tales of Merlin and Taliesin,[3] but no mention of prophecies is made in this report. If the amount of prophetic verse surviving in Welsh manuscripts is any indication — and there are at least fifty manuscripts, many containing numerous prophecies — then the view of the Welsh as susceptible to the effects of prophecy is one which needs to be taken seriously.

The most comprehensive study of Welsh prophecy is M. E. Griffiths' survey, *Early Vaticination in Welsh with English Parallels*,[4] published about fifty years ago, and much of what she says remains valid. The purpose of this paper is to consider prophetic verse in the context of Welsh folk tradition and also to reassess the function of Welsh prophetic verse with this added dimension. Since Griffiths' monograph was published, a number of vaticinatory poems have been edited,[5] most notably those attributed to Merlin.[6] He, of course, is one of the most popular figures to whom poetry of this kind is ascribed, although recently a great deal of work has been done on the *Book of Taliesin*[7] and the *Tale of Taliesin*.[8] Taliesin is another important figure on whom prophecy was fostered. In addition the historical situation in Wales in the late medieval and

52

Tudor periods has received careful analysis,[9] and it is now possible to give a clearer picture of the contemporary social milieu and the cultural background within which these poems were written.

Griffiths suggested that Welsh prophecy was largely a native poetic tradition before the fifteenth century. Its roots were very old and depended ultimately on the function of the earliest bards as both prophets and poets. Prophecy in medieval Wales was essentially political in nature and arose, in its early stages, out of the struggle of the Welsh against the Saxons, and this struggle continued during the period of Norman occupation. This expressed itself primarily in the belief in a returning hero such as Arthur. In subsequent centuries prophecy was used by the Welsh princes in their dynastic struggles, reaching a climax, both in intensity and in the amount of verse produced, during the Tudor struggle in the fifteenth century.[10]

Griffiths' conclusions have been more or less accepted by subsequent writers, although no one has attempted such a comprehensive view. It seems sensible, then, to use her as a starting point in any new attempt to consider the development and function of vaticinatory verse in medieval and Tudor Wales. With this in mind, it will be convenient to divide the discussion into five sections following the general outline of Griffiths' argument. The first point to consider, or rather reconsider, is the relation of the existing prophecies to the prophetic function of the early bard. The second is the function of the expected deliverer, in particular, the lack of Arthur as a deliverer figure in the poetry. The third is the influence of messianism and apocalytic writing on Welsh vaticination. Fourth is its use as political propaganda. And last — a point not considered by Griffiths — is the extent to which this poetry can be considered part of the tradition and folklore of Welsh culture.

The first point is the relation of the medieval material to the poetry of the early bards. The emphasis here has been on the continuity between early Celtic and medieval Welsh tradition. Most scholars are in agreement that part of the early poet's function was that of seer and prophet and that this function was an ancient heritage among Celtic peoples going back ultimately to the position of the Druids.[11] Griffiths suggests that medieval Welsh vaticination followed in this tradition. Certainly it is true that the Celtic poet was more than just a maker of verse,[12] but to see Welsh prophecies as directly linked to this is too simple and obscures some interesting features of the tradition.

Taliesin and Merlin were undoubtedly regarded as prophets at an early period.[13] The well-known reference in *Historia Brittonum* attests to Taliesin's historicity, and he is acknowledged as the author of the genuine heroic-verse included in the *Book of Taliesin*.[14] However, there is a long

gap between the early elegiac material and the later prophecies attributed
to him, and he is depicted as a magician as well as a prophet (more the
former than the latter in fact) in the narratives attached to him in the *Tale
of Taliesin*. It is interesting to compare material attributed to Taliesin with
that attributed to Aneirin, another historical poet mentioned in *Historia
Brittonum*. Material ascribed to Aneirin is not prophecy, but proverbial
wisdom made up of gnomic material together with some very obscure
heroic and historic references.[15] If prophecy was an intrinsic or even
common function of early poets, then the distinction between these two
historical bards is difficult to account for. Earlier scholarship, in particular
the pioneering work of Ifor Williams,[16] depended on establishing clear,
or at least credible, historical connections between bodies of material and
approached the text in a rather literal way. Recent scholarship has begun
to take account of the importance of legend, and even folklore, in shaping
historical tradition,[17] and this is particularly suited to understanding the
development of vaticinatory verse in Wales. The emphasis of this approach
is not just on historical development, it also considers how tradition adapts
itself to social and political pressures and to popular movements. The
development of Welsh vaticination may reflect, not so much the actual
experiences of invasion and loss of independence, but an interpretation
of history in which Wales was viewed as a country unjustly deprived of
its land, but whose wrongs would eventually be avenged. Taliesin and
Merlin may have acquired a reputation for prophecy quite independent
of the vaticinatory tradition whereas Aneirin did not, nor for that
matter, the other presumably historical poets mentioned in the *Historia
Brittonum*, none of whose poetry has apparently survived and who have
almost completely passed out of tradition as well. This approach does not
lead to conclusions radically different from Griffiths as far as the poetry is
concerned, but it may be useful in regards to Merlin whose historicity is
still disputed,[18] although he was certainly regarded by later Welsh poets
as a real poet and a prophet.[19] There is not space for an adequate analysis of
the figure of Merlin, but it is worth noting in passing that Merlin in Welsh
tradition is associated with prophecy and his character as 'wild man' is
used as motivation for this role, while the analogous figure of Suibne in
Irish and Gaelic tradition remains primarily a wild man with very little
material of a prophetic nature being associated with him.[20] The tale which
explains how Taliesin gained his powers is a common international tale
(The Magician and His Pupil) which is found in most Celtic countries
connected with various figures who were thought to have magic powers.
However, Wales is the only country where the figure associated with this
tale also has a substantial body of prophecy attached to his name.[21]

The second point which needs to be considered is the relation of vaticinatory verse to the expectation of a deliverer. This is an element common to all this poetry and, considering the obscurity and abundance of the verse, it is a remarkably stable element. In the later Tudor poetry, the deliverer is often identified as Henry Tudor, 'mab darogan', the son of prophecy, who is coming back to fulfil the prophecies. The traditional names of the deliverers are Owain, Cynan and Cadwaladyr. Arthur is not a frequent deliverer figure in Welsh vaticinatory verse. Arthur's return occurs more frequently in a narrative context. An important feature of the narrative tradition, and one at odds with the prophetic verse, is that the tales indicate the time for his return is not yet. In narratives, Arthur and his knights are told to sleep again, whereas the poems nearly always predict that the time of the deliverer is at hand. The relative absence of Arthur in poetry may reflect a difference between native Welsh tradition and the more international strain represented by Geoffrey of Monmouth. It may be that poetic prophecy in Welsh continued to draw on a wider native tradition in which Arthur was not the only hope of Britain.

A more commonly expected deliverer in poetry is Cadwaladyr, the last king of the Britons,[22] and the more problematic Owain. The earliest reference to Owain seems to be in the 'Cyfoesi Merddin' found in the Red Book of Hergest.[23] Who he was is unclear, but he is a very popular figure. Considering the importance of Welsh leaders with this name — Owain Gwynedd during the time of Henry II, Owain Lawgoch during the fourteenth century and Owain Glyn Dwr during the reign of Henry IV — this is not surprising, and no doubt the composition of poems featuring Owain was actively encouraged by his namesakes. Owain vab Urien is the most likely source for this figure, as he was one of the *Gwŷr y Gogledd*, northern figures both heroic and historic who became assimilated into Welsh tradition.[24] The use of Cadwaladyr may reveal something about the dynamic that lies behind Welsh prophecy. Prophecy contains a number of motifs which symbolise a reversal of fortune for the defeated, in particular the return of a hero and a victorious battle both foreshadowed by numerous signs. One of the functions of Welsh prophecy undoubtedly was its ability to sustain a view of Wales as a country deprived unjustly of its heritage, like Cadwaladyr, and struggling to regain it.[25]

Because of the amount of material and the difficulty of dating specific poems, it is virtually impossible to establish firm criteria for classification, but it does seem that the Merlin material which appears mostly in the twelfth century *Black Book of Carmarthen* frequently invokes Cynan and Cadwaladyr as deliverers of the Welsh nation. The vaticinatory poems in the *Book of Taliesin* (c.1275) mention Owain, although Cynan and Cadwaladyr are the heroes in *Armes Prydein*, perhaps the earliest Welsh prophecy included in this manuscript. Verses written between 1200 and

C

1400 outside these two important sources are frequently attributed to poets other than Merlin and Taliesin. Among the most common are Adda Fras, Goronwy Ddu, both Anglesey poets, Y Bergam who came from Maelor, and most important Rhys Fardd (Y Bardd Bach) from Oystermouth near Swansea. Clear references to historical persons such as Owain Lawgoch (d. 1378) and Owain Glyn Dwr (c. 1354–1416) occur in these later verses. After 1400, Geoffrey's type of prophecy becomes more prominent. This is notable since Geoffrey's work had been well-known for some time, and Welsh prophecy seems to have retained its character despite this. At this period, Welsh prophecy became more open to outside influence generally and translations of English and Latin prophecies began to appear.[26] Coincident with the period of the Wars of the Roses were the most numerous and in many ways the most striking of Welsh prophecies, the *cywyddau brud*. Written in cywydd metre by poets like Dafydd Llwyd of Mathafarn, they incorporate many of the earlier elements of Welsh prophecy together with elements from Geoffrey of Monmouth and from European tradition, and they are written with considerable political acumen and poetic skill.[27] These poets produced poems which are completely literary on one level, but still remain in touch with the traditional roots of prophecy.

Popular movements are often influential in shaping literary tradition. The rise of a phenomenon known as messianism in Europe in the later Middle Ages[28] certainly influenced Welsh prophecy, in particular the development of the theme of the returning deliverer. This is noticeable as early as the end of the thirteenth century after the death of the last native Welsh prince. Some prophecies give the name Llewelyn to the expected deliverer,[29] and these may have been written to glorify the princes of the house of Gwynedd such as Llewelyn ap Iorwerth and Llewellyn ap Gruffudd himself, the last prince of Wales. The importance of 1282 as a turning point in Welsh history is still a matter of debate.[30] Certainly the significance of the date as a symbol for the end of Welsh independence has increased under the influence of modern ideas of Welsh nationhood. It is not too much to suggest that the romantic view of Wales so prominent in the last century often makes it extremely difficult to assess earlier material.[31] The elegies written to Llewelyn ap Gruffydd immediately after his death show an awareness of his special role but no hint of a miraculous return.[32] On the other hand, enough ambitious Welsh princelings were still alive, some of whom could even claim connection with the house of Gwynedd, and prophecies continued to be written predicting the triumph of a Welsh prince. In fact, soon after this time, there was an intensification of interest in prophecy and an increase in the number of poems being written. From the thirteenth century onwards,

Welsh prophecies focus more and more on the imminent return of a deliverer. Earlier prophecies had concentrated on portents similar to those thought to herald Doomsday, signs in nature such as eclipses or rivers running blood. Later prophecies began to predict the time was at hand, and by the period of the *cywyddau brud*, specific historical figures were being singled out. Undoubtedly social and political developments in Wales account for this change of focus to some extent, but the rising tide of messianism in Europe also shaped Welsh prophecy at this time. Joachim of Fiore has been suggested as one of the messianic writers who may have influenced Welsh prophecies. Certainly Joachim's works were widely known, but the phrase 'mab y dyn' which Griffiths relates to an English prophecy influenced by Joachim's works[33] occurs in St Matthew's Gospel and in apocryphal apocalyptic books which would also have been widely read. The only specific mention of Joachim is rather late,[34] and his direct influence on Welsh prophecy was probably not great. However, messianism provided a model which could be grafted on very easily to existing themes in Welsh prophecy since it predicted a dramatic change in the order of reality and a spiritual redemption of history by a returning 'messianic' figure. This idea, linked to the sense of cultural victimisation articulated so clearly in the earlier prophecies, could have produced a potent combination that might account for the change of tone in Welsh prophecies. Messianic prophecies have a mystical and religious tone which is absent in Welsh until the Tudor period. Before this, the direction of Welsh poems is towards the triumph of the Welsh as a nation over their enemies.

By the end of the period, some Tudor historians at least were thinking in terms of a distinct group of people linked by common culture and language,[35] but the extent of truly national consciousness during the medieval period is not clear. Often faction rather than nation is the appropriate word, and modern Welsh nationalism has sometimes over-emphasised the idea of early nationhood.[36] Nevertheless, the imagery in the prophecies refers to a nation which has lost its rightful patrimony and is struggling against an oppressor. The special characteristics of the poetry are also established and, although every poem may not contain every theme, they remain constant throughout the genre. There is always a reference to enemies (the Saxons and the 'men of Lloegr' are the most popular); realistic descriptions of battles, often at specific places, but entirely fictional; lists of evils to come based on weather predictions, natural disturbances and signs like those before Doomsday and, of course, the deliverer or eventual triumph of the Welsh nation. Particularly as regards the later prophecies, the *cywyddau brud*, the genre is that of self-conscious poetry rather than popular prophecy.

These poems are less a prediction of the future than they are a spur to action and were presumably directed at the relatively small audience of prince and nobles. The poems by this time have real not traditional authors, and the eventual choice by these authors of Henry Tudor as *mab darogan* shows an awareness of the realities of politics also absent before this time.[37]

A constant problem with prophetic poetry is the lateness of the manuscripts. The fact that so much material of this type survives tells us a great deal about the scribes and collectors of the sixteenth and seventeenth centuries who compiled these manuscripts. They clearly recognised the importance of the material and also that Welsh culture needed to be preserved,[38] and their choices inevitably affect our perceptions of prophetic verse. Even if we limit ourselves to the period when the texts were being composed, however, dating is not easy, and a description of the significance of the material is very difficult. Griffiths points out that many prophecies contain much earlier material,[39] and Ifor Williams suggests that elements of the prophecies in the *Book of Taliesin* are much earlier than the surviving texts.[40] The popular aspect of the prophecies is even harder to chronicle. While it is undoubtedly the case that prophecies circulated orally in some form, and that written prophecies incorporated some oral and popular elements, this seems a disappointingly vague conclusion about what must have been an extremely important element in the development of the genre. However, a knowledge of Welsh folklore can be of help in understanding this aspect of the tradition. Probably the earliest of Welsh prophecies to have been preserved is the prophecy of the Two Dragons in *Historia Brittonum*, while the earliest poetic text may be *Armes Prydein* which Sir Ifor Williams dates to the early tenth century.[41] Clearly scribes were selective and much material has been lost, but the picture of Welsh prophecy even in its more popular aspects is not irretrievably blurred.

The prophecy of the Two Dragons is one of the best known of Welsh prophecies. It first appears in narrative form in *Historia Brittonum*. It tells the story of Vortigern whose tower will not stand until two dragons are unearthed and their actions interpreted by the boy Emrys (Ambrosius). This type of prophecy is very similar to the traditional interpretation of dreams. Dream prophecies are a popular type of prophecy. During the Middle Ages, the Dream of Adam Davy was widely known in England,[42] and in Wales Merlin's interpretation of the dreams of his sister. The latter is particularly interesting because it is preserved in Geoffrey's *Vita Merlini*,[43] in Elis Gruffudd's *Chronicl*[44] in the early sixteenth century and, quite amazingly, as a late folktale.[45] In the Two Dragons, however, the event is depicted as real, not a dream, while the format is different from poetic prophecies, and the source behind *Historia Brittonum* may have been a narrative. The story appears again in the tale of *Lludd and Llefelys* in the *Mabinogion* and in a Welsh translation of Geoffrey's *Historia Regum Brittaniae* (National Library of Wales Ms. Llanstefan I).[46] This version is dependent on Geoffrey but closer to *Historia Brittonum*. The content of the prophecy suggests that a sense of historical destiny which predicted eventual triumph for the nation was certainly present at an early period, and the variation in the few surviving texts as well as numerous references to the prophecy in poetry[47] indicate that it was widely known. The interpretation of dreams as symbolic of future events remains extremely common in folk tradition, although as a folklore phenomenon it usually relates to events in a person's life and not to the destiny of nations.[48]

One of the earliest sources for British tradition is Gildas' *De Excidio Britanniae*.[49] He, however, says nothing about British prophecies, although he claims that the Saxons had a prophecy predicting that they would triumph in Britain. Geoffrey of Monmouth is a rich, if ecletic, source for prophetic tradition. The *Historia Regum Britanniae* and *Vita* and *Prophetiae Merlini* (1136–1148) use Welsh materials, probably gathered at second hand despite his claims to have used a book written in the British tongue. The prophecy of the Two Dragons he links to Merlin, and in this form it became known as 'Proffwydoliaeth Fawr' in Welsh tradition.[50] Arthur becomes the central deliverer although Cadwaladyr is mentioned. Grafted onto the Welsh style of prophecy which addressed natural objects like birch trees, apple trees and little pigs is the method typical of Geoffrey in which 'totem' animals are used to signify the figures to which the prophecies refer. Here I would disagree with M. E. Griffiths who suggests that Geoffrey was influenced by the use of animals in Welsh prophecy.[51] What imagery occurs in Welsh is not used in the same way as Geoffrey where it clearly points to the identity of the person in the prophecy. Although he uses material in a highly original way, Geoffrey reflects what was obviously happening elsewhere in Welsh tradition. A distinct view of Wales and its place in history was beginning to emerge. The heroic tradition began to be seen as an old tradition reflecting the beginning of Welsh culture. Geoffrey puts this into a European context by making the Welsh descendants of the Trojans, whereas some of the *Mabinogion* stories linked together the ancient heroes with gods and goddesses in a glorious Welsh past. Arthur's humorous comment in *Breuddwyd Rhonawbwy* about the smallness of today's men compared with the heroes of the past sums up the attitude very accurately. The glories of the past were not lost forever, and the prophecies look forward to the resurgence of Wales.

Giraldus Cambrensis' work contains a great deal of information about the nature of prophecy in the Middle Ages. In it, he describes the *awenyddion* who go into a trance-like state and prophesy, their utterances being written down.[52] He also mentions several famous prophecies himself.[53] By the twelfth century it is quite likely that material had begun to be recorded; indeed the *Black Book of Carmarthen* is not all that long after Giraldus. Giraldus includes a number of prophetic incidents such as the fact that the birds singing over Llyn Syfaddan will herald the arrival of a true Welsh prince, and that if a freckled prince were to cross a bridge at Nant Pentcarn, Wales would suffer, and of course he describes events which allegedly fulfilled these, and other, prophecies.[54] Giraldus' comments about the *awenyddion* may have been based on an earlier source and not something he himself witnessed, but they do illustrate contemporary beliefs. He himself asserts that spirits communicate with men before important events.[55] The incidents he cites may reflect something of the actual use of prophecy. Although no texts are given, they demonstrate a pattern of portent and fulfilment, and clearly if prophecies lie behind these incidents, they must have been short, uncomplicated, and able to be applied to actual events.

There are a few Welsh references to prophecy and its use. The *History of Gruffydd ap Cynon* invokes prophetic material to support the importance of this prince, although he is not viewed as an expected deliverer. The *History*, written in the late eleventh or early twelfth century, actually quotes four lines of a prophecy which it ascribes to Merlin[56] but which Griffiths points out is very close to a passage in a poem in the *Book of Taliesin*.[57] This exemplifies another problem in medieval prophetic tradition, namely determining how and in what form prophecies circulated. Manuscripts devoted in whole or in part to prophecies abound, and there is the testimony of men such as Giraldus and Higden that the Welsh were much influenced by them. However, as they do not show a great degree of variation from manuscript to manuscript, it is difficult to see how such long and complex poems would circulate orally. Undoubtedly poets were encouraged to write this material by ambitious patrons, and undoubtedly they recited these poems which were in turn memorised by other poets. However, material certainly circulated at a popular level as well. The incidents related by Giraldus and the use of prophecy in the *History of Gruffydd ap Cynon* give an idea of how prophecy functioned during the medieval period, and from these references we can assume that oral prophecies may have circulated as short, relatively simple verses with a format of portent and result.

Many folk beliefs and in particular signs believed to foreshadow death are similar to prophecy in that seemingly disconnected events are linked as if they were cause and effect. Death omens such as the *toili* and the *corpse candle* are the most common phenomena foreshadowing death in Welsh folk tradition. As death affects the integrity of small communities, the ability to exercise some control over it, in this case by linking the death with some event which is thought to anticipate it, would have an important function in community life.[58] T. G. Jones was the first to point out similarities in the functions of political and folk prophecy. He was inclined to see prophecy as the work of disordered and confused minds, while modern scholarship has stressed the positive function of such phenomena in society. Despite the difference in approach, T. G. Jones accurately catches the tone of the prophecies as 'obsession by the past and the future, of an atmosphere of expectation, in which everything is portentous, in which anything may happen at any moment.[59]

The connection between vaticination and popular prophecy is clearly one of interaction. It is virtually impossible to establish specific sources for the popular elements, but it is quite likely that at least one technique of composition used popular prophecies of the type we have been discussing as building blocks on which to string or expand prophetic poems that could be adapted to fit the circumstances of a particular time or the reputation of a particular prince. Weather lore illustrates very clearly both the connection between folk belief and prophecy and the special register of prophecy. Most weather beliefs are expressed as short aphoristic sayings which name a specific condition of the weather and what happens as a result, a format very similar to the portent/fulfilment of the prophecy. When this material is collected, the informant will often give an instance in which the belief was borne out by the weather of a particular season or year.[60] Being able to predict weather is obviously important in agricultural communities, and most weather lore is based on relatively accurate observations of the natural world. For example, a flowery April means a shortage of apples and plums. Prophecy, however, usually anticipates a disruption in the natural order: for example, thunder in February predicts a marvel during the summer or a sun with smaller orbs emanating from it denotes misfortune and destruction. The first could have some basis in reality, too many blossoms could result in less fruit, but the beliefs about thunder and the sun are a different kind of prediction. Portents like these almost always predict ill-luck of some kind. In a sense they try to anticipate fate, but hardly ever in such a way that it can be avoided. In their attempt to predict fate, folk beliefs are closest to prophecy. The messianic return of the Welsh hero is somewhat untypical in this respect, in that it will have a positive outcome. T. G. Jones recalls a conversation one summer, when red berries were unusually plentiful on the yew and holly trees, with an old man in Cardiganshire who told him that this was a sign of bloodshed to come. The time was August 1914.[61]

Clearly the dividing line between this kind of folk belief and the kind of prophecy we have been discussing is very fine.

The work of M. E. Griffiths provided the starting point for this discussion, and many of her insights into the nature of prophecy remain valid. The themes of deliverer and of eventual triumph for the Welsh are constant throughout the tradition and stamp it with a unique character. The importance of external influences such as other European prophecies and of the messianic view of history was perhaps stronger than Griffiths realised, but in no way does this dilute the uniqueness or the importance of the genre for Welsh literary and historical tradition. The role of folklore in Welsh prophetic poetry — what I have called the popular elements of the tradition — was crucial. Elements of folk prophecy are included in the poems, although it is very hard to positively identify and isolate these elements. However, the most important contribution of folklore is that it provided the background from which vaticinatory verse developed. The same belief system that supports weather lore, and omens of all kinds, also supports prophecy. However complex the later *cywyddau brud* become, they are never just conceits: even the later poems retain their connection with folk tradition in that they depend ultimately on the categories of folk prophecy to give them shape and meaning.

NOTES

1. William Shakespeare, *The History of Richard II*, Act II, sc. iv.

2. Ralph of Higdon, *Polychronicon*, Rolls Series vol. I, 408–10.

3. I. Williams, 'Hen Chwedlau', *Trans.Hon.Soc. Cymm.* (1946–47), 28.

4. M. E. Griffiths, *Early Vaticination in Welsh with English Parallels*, ed. T. Gwynn Jones (Cardiff, 1937).

5. See especially the work of R. Wallis Evans, 'Prophetic Poetry', in *A Guide to Welsh Literature*, vol. 2 A. O. H. Jarman and Gwillym Rees Hughes (Swansea, 1979) 278–297; 'Tair Cerdd Ddarogan', *Bull.Board.Celt.Stud.*, 10 (1939–41), 44–52: 'Y Broffwydoliaeth Fawr a 'r Broffwydoliaeth Fer', *Bull.Board.Celt.Stud.*, 22 (1966/68), 119–21.

6. A. O. H. Jarman, 'The Welsh Myrddin Poems', in *Arthurian Literature in the Middle Ages* ed. R. S. Loomis (Oxford, 1958); *The Legend of Myrddin* (Cardiff, 1958); *Ymddiddan Myrddin a Thaliesin* (Cardiff, 1967); 'Early Stages in the Development of the Myrddin Legend', in *Astudiaethau ar yr Hengerdd* (ed. R. Bromwich and R. B. Jones, Cardiff, 1978), 326–49; *Merlin, An inaugural lecture* delivered at University College Cardiff, 1959 (1970); Eurys I. Rowlands, 'Myrddin ar Bawl', *Llen Cymru* 5 (1958/59), 87–88; for a view of Merlin as an historical poet see Tolstoy, 'Merlinus Redivivus', *Stud.Celt.*, 18/19 (1983/84), 11–29.

7. Marged Haycock, 'Preiddeu Annwn and the Figure of Taliesin', *Stud.Celt.* 18/19 (1983/84), 52–78.

8. J. M. Wood, 'The Elphin Section of *Hanes Taliesin*', *Etud.Celt.* 18 (1981), 229–244; 'Versions of *Hanes Taliesin* by Owen John and Lewis Morris', *Bull.Board.Celt.Stud.* 29

(1981/82), 285–294;, 'The Folklore Background of the Gwion Bach Section of *Hanes Taliesin*', *Bull.Board.Celt.Stud.* 29 (1981/82), 621–634; Patrick Ford, 'A Fragment of the *Hanes Taliesin* by Llewelyn Sion', *Etud.Celt.* 14 (1975), 451–59.

9. S. B. Chrimes, *Henry VII* (London, 1972). For a more popular analysis see David Rees, *The Son of Prophecy, Henry Tudor's Road to Bosworth* (Black Raven Press, 1985).

10. Griffiths (note 4 above), 9–10, 54, 215–18.

11. Basil Clarke, *Life of Merlin, Geoffrey of Monmouth Vita Merlini* (Cardiff, 1973); Tolstoy, *The Quest for Merlin* (London, 1985); J. E. Caerwyn Williams, *Traddodiad Llenyddol Iwerddon* (Cardiff, 1958); 'The Court Poet in Medieval Ireland' Sir John Rhys Memorial Lectures 1971 (London, 1971); F. N. Robinson, 'Satirists and Enchanters in Early Irish Literature', in *Studies in the History of Religions, Essays presented to C. H. Toy* (New York, 1912). The list of writers who have considered the nature and function of the Celtic poet is extensive, and I have only included a selection relevant to Welsh prophecy.

12. J. E. Caerwyn Williams, 'The Court Poet in Medieval Ireland', Sir John Rhys Memorial Lectures 1971, 16, 22–29.

13. R. Bromwich, 'Y Cynfeirdd a 'r Traddodiad Cymraeg', *Bull. Board. Celt. Stud.* 22 (66–68), 30–37; Griffiths (note 4 above), 74.

14. *Historia Brittonum* ed. A. Wade-Evans (London, 1938), 80; I. Williams, *Beginnings of Welsh Poetry* ed. Rachel Bromwich (Cardiff, 1972), 43; *The Poems of Taliesin* trans. J. E. Caerwyn Williams (Dublin, 1968).

15. I. Williams, *Canu Aneirin* (Cardiff, 1970), 50–57.

16. I. Williams (note 14 above); K. H. Jackson, 'On the Northern British Section in Nennius', in *Celt and Saxon, Studies in the Early British Border* ed. N. K. Chadwick *et al* (Cambridge, 1963), 20–62.

17. T. Gwynn Jones, *Welsh Folklore and Folk-Custom* 1930 (London, 1979), 138–39; although he considers the material from a folklorist's point of view, he still stresses the connection with the druids; D. N. Dumville, 'Sub Roman Britain: History and Legend', *History* 57 (1977), 186; 'Paleographical Considerations on the dating of Early Welsh Verse', *Bull. Board. Celt. Stud.* 27 (1976/78), 249–51 considers some of the linguistic and paleographical problems in dating this material.

18. A. O. H. Jarman, 'A Oedd Myrddin yn Fardd Hanesyddol', *Stud.Celt.* 10/11 (1975–76), 182–87; Griffiths (note 4 above); 74 seems to accept Merlin's historicity, and most recently this argument has been restated by N. Tolstoy in 'Merlinus Redivivus', *Stud.Celt.* 18/19 (1983/4).

19. R. Bromwich (note 13 above), 34.

20. Brian R. Frykenburg, 'The Wild Man in Ecclesiastical Legend and Tradition' (unpublished M.A. thesis, Univ. of Edinburgh, 1981) gives a detailed description of the wild man legend in Celtic tradition. For a specific analysis of the role in Welsh tradition, see Eurys I. Rowlands, 'Myrddin Wyllt', *Llen Cymru* 4 (1956/57), 117–19.

21. David Rees (note 9 above), 98–109; W. Garmon Jones, 'Welsh Nationalism and Henry Tudor', *Trans.Hon.Soc.Cymm.* (1917–18) 1–59.

22. R. Bromwich, *Trioedd Ynys Prydein*, The Welsh Triads (rev. ed. Cardiff 1978), 292–93; see also G. Goetinck, 'The Blessed Heroes', *Stud.Celt.* 20/21 (1985/86), 87–109 for a discussion of the significance of Cadwalydyr in relation to Welsh identity and destiny.

23. Griffiths (note 4 above), 100; *The Poetry in the Red Book of Hergest* (Llanbedrog, 1911), col. 581, lines 13–15.

24. I. Williams, *Beginnings of Welsh Poetry*, 49; Bromwich (note 22 above), 479–83.

25. G. Goetinck, 'The Blessed Heroes', *Stud.Celt.* 20/21 (1985/86), 95, 100–02.

26. Griffiths (note 4 above), 170–72; R. Wallis Evans, 'Proffwydoliaeth Banastyr o Brydein Fawr, *Bull. Board. Celt. Stud. 22 (1966/68), 121–24.*

27. R. Wallis Evans, 'Prophetic Poetry', 285–296; W. Leslie Richards, *Gwaith Dafydd Llwyd o Fathafarn* (Cardiff, 1964); G. Glanmor Williams, 'Proffwydoliaeth, Prydyddiaeth a Pholitics yn yr Oesodd Canol', *Taliesin* 1968, 31–39.

28. Norman Cohn, *The Pursuit of the Millenium* (new. ed., New York, 1970); Constance Bullock-Davies, 'Espectare Arturum: Arthur and the Messianic Hope', *Bull.Board.Celt. Stud.* 29 (80/82), 432.

29. Griffiths (note 4 above), 164, 166–167.

30. Glyn Roberts, 'The Significance of 1282', *Wales through the Ages* I, 128–37; A. D. Carr 'The Historical Background, 1282–1550' (note 5 above), II, 13.

31. Prys Morgan, 'From Death to a View: The Hunt for the Welsh Past in the Romantic Period', in *The Invention of Tradition* (ed. E. Hobsbawn and T. Ranger, Cambridge, 1984), 46–47, 63.

32. T. G. Jones (note 17 above), 140; Griffiths (note 4 above), 'The Death of Llewelyn ap Gruffydd, *Bull. Board. Celt. Stud.* 15 (1953), 207–09. This article contains an edition of a contemporary letter describing the death of Llewelyn from the English point of view.

33. Griffiths (note 4 above), 170–71. The prophecy referred to is 'The Lily, the Lion and the Son of Man'.

34. National Library of Wales Ms. Peniarth 50, 169, c.1350–65.

35. For example, Elis Gruffudd's *Chronicl y Wech Oesodd*, National Library of Wales Ms. 5276D.

36. Prys Morgan (note 31 above).

37. Wallis Evans (note 27 above), 287–296.

38. Prys Morgan (note 31 above).

39. Griffiths (note 4 above), 100, 129.

40. I. Williams, 'Chwedl Taliesin' (Cardiff, 1957).

41. *Armes Prydein o Lyfr Taliesin* (ed. I. Williams, Cardiff, 1955).

42. Rupert Taylor, *The Political Prophecy in England, 1911* (New York, 1967).

43. Basil Clarke, *Life of Merlin, Geoffrey of Monmouth Vita Merlini.*

44. Thomas Jones, 'The Story of Myrddin and the Five Dreams of Gwendydd in the Chronicle of Elis Gruffudd', *Et.Celt.* viii (1959), 315–45.

45. R. Wallis Evans, 'Pum Breuddwyd Gwendydd', *Bull. Board. Celt. Stud.* 12 (1946/48), 19–22.

46. *Cyfranc Lludd a Llefelys* (ed. Brynley F. Roberts, Dublin, 1975) xxxviii, xxxv.

47. R. Wallis Evans, 'Y Broffwydoliaeth Fawr a'r Broffwydoliaeth Fer', *Bull. Board. Celt. Stud.* 22 (1966/68); Griffiths (note 4 above), 30–31, 67–68.

48. See tape recordings and transcripts held at the Welsh Folk Museum, St Fagans, Cardiff for interviews with Welsh-speaking informants on the interpretations of dreams.

49. Gildas, *The Ruin of Britain* and other documents, *Arthurian Period Sources*, vol. 7 (ed. and trans. Michael Winterbottom, London, 1978); Griffiths (note 4 above), 30.

50. R. Wallis Evans (note 47 above); Griffiths (note 4 above), 30.

51. Griffiths (note 4 above), 74.

52. Giraldus Cambrensis, *The Itinerary through Wales and the Description of Wales* (trans. R. C. Hoare 1908, London, New York, 1976) 179.

53. Ibid., *Description*, cap. xvi, 180.

54. Ibid., *Itinerary*, cap. ii, 32.

55. Ibid., *Itinerary*, cap. v, 55.

56. *Historia Gruffudd vab Kenan* ed. D. Simon Evans (Cardiff, 1977), 5–7.

57. Griffiths (note 4 above), 106–7, 121-22; J. Gwenogvryn Evans, *The Text of the Book of Taliesin* (Llandbedrog, 1911), 70–71, lines 25–26.

58. T. Gwynn Jones (note 17 above), 140.

59. My thanks to Dr Anne Williams for her helpful suggestions about weather predictions.

60. Marie Trevelyan, *Folklore and Folk Stories of Wales* (London, 1909), 118–124, 244–264. See holding of the Welsh Folk Museum, St Fagans, Cardiff for interviews with Welsh-speaking informants on weather beliefs and seasonal lore.

61. T. Gwynn Jones, (note 17 above), 167.

5

The Seer's Thumb

Hilda Ellis Davidson

The motif of the placing of the thumb in the mouth as a means of acquiring wisdom is found in the medieval literature of both Scandinavia and Ireland. It poses some problems which are worth considering, since this ritual gesture, long remembered in popular tradition, may throw light on the interaction of Norse and Irish lore concerning the relations of the seer with the supernatural world. In addition to written sources we need to consider evidence from folklore and iconography.

The seer plays an important part in Norse and Irish tradition.[1] The Norse seeress or *völva* beholds from her high seat matters hidden from common knowledge, and may reveal the destinies of children, momentous events to come, or secrets of the past. There are memories also of the seer known as the *thul* who gave advice to kings and interpreted dreams and runes; he also sat on a high seat to reveal the past and the future. In Irish tradition the seer-poet, the *fili*, similarly predicts what is to come and explores secrets of the past, helping kings and warriors and foretelling the fate of royal houses and mighty heroes. Poems are preserved in both literatures which are represented as the utterances of seers and seeresses.

Youthful heroes needed certain kinds of knowledge as well as fighting skills, and a seer might play an important part in a young prince's education. The tale of Sigurd the Volsung is told in a fourteenth-century Icelandic Saga, *Völsunga Saga*, known to contain material from earlier heroic poems. Some of these poems survive in a manuscript book of the thirteenth century known as the *Codex Regius*, one of the treasures of Iceland. The medieval German version of the tale is that of the hero Siegfried in the *Nibelungenlied*, and the tragedy of the great hero's early death became a major theme in medieval northern literature. Here, however, I am concerned only with the early part of Sigurd's life and with his first great achievement, the slaying of a dragon.

The existing Icelandic sources go back to the thirteenth century, but Sigurd is said to be the son of Sigmund, one of the greatest of Odin's heroes, famous in earlier Icelandic and Anglo-Saxon literature. According to *Völsunga Saga* Sigurd was born after his father had been killed in battle, due to the intervention of Odin himself, who shattered the sword which he himself had given to Sigmund years before. Sigurd's mother made a second marriage, and she kept the pieces of the broken blade for her son. The boy Sigurd was taught by Regin, a smith with supernatural powers whose family could take on various shapes; his brother Fafnir had become a dragon and guarded a great golden treasure in a mound, which Regin longed to possess. Odin showed favour to Sigurd and gave him a wonderful horse, while Regin reforged his father's broken sword and then egged him on to kill the dragon and win the gold. He told him to dig a pit from which he could stab Fafnir from below, since dragons are only vulnerable in the belly, but Regin intended Sigurd to perish in the flow of blood so that he would be left in possession of the treasure. However, Odin intervened and told Sigurd to dig a series of pits so that the blood would be distributed among them, and Sigurd dealt Fafnir his death blow. Regin drank some of the blood and then told Sigurd to roast the dragon's heart for him to eat. Sigurd did as he was told, but while the heart was roasting he touched it to see if it was done, burned his thumb (or finger) and put it in his mouth.[2] Immediately he understood the speech of birds, and heard the nuthatches on the tree above warning him against the teacherous Regin who intended his death. Sigurd drew his sword and cut off Regin's head. Then he loaded the treasure on to his horse and rode away to new adventures.

While no written versions of this tale are known before the thirteenth century, the various episodes of it are clearly depicted on a number of stones of the late tenth and early eleventh centuries from northern England and the Isle of Man (Fig. 1).[3] Sigurd is depicted with his thumb in his mouth, while we are also shown the forging of the sword, the slaying of the dragon from beneath, the heart roasting over a fire, two birds on a tree, the beheading of the smith, and the horse with a load on its back. These carvings are mostly on Christian memorial stones commemorating the dead. Later in the twelfth and thirteenth centuries, the same sequence of scenes was carved skilfully on doorposts of Norwegian stave churches, helping to interpret worn parts of the carved stones. A different method of presentation was adopted for a rock carving at Jäder, Södermanland, in Sweden (Fig. 2), where the dragon's serpentine body forms a border with runes inscribed on it; the hero stabs it from below, while inside the other motifs are arranged in a group, the figure of a man roasting the heart in slices on a stick, with his thumb in his mouth, being especially predominant.

Evidently the tale was known in Viking England before AD 1000 and

Fig. 1. Two top panels of cross shaft from Halton, near Lancaster. The lower one shows the roasting of the heart in slices over a fire and a man with his thumb in his mouth, and the upper one two birds on a stylised tree (drawing by Brian Megaw in *Manx Museum Journal*, vol. 5, 1942).

Fig. 2. Rasmus rock, Jäder, Södermanland, Sweden, showing man with thumb in mouth and slice of heart on a stick, together with birds on tree and headless smith. The stabbing of the dragon is depicted below (drawing by Eileen Aldworth).

was soon afterwards depicted in Norway and Sweden, although we do not know what name was given to the hero. According to the Anglo-Saxon poem *Beowulf* Sigmund also slew a dragon and gained a treasure, but few details are given. Certainly the incidents of the slaying and the roasting of the heart, with the thumb in the mouth of the hero, became extremely popular. By the thirteenth century the hero was recognised as Sigurd, and episodes from the later part of the Volsung saga are also depicted. The roasting scenes may have appeared on wall hangings also, since a verse by a poet of the eleventh century at the court of Olaf II of Norway describes a tapestry in the king's hall which shows 'a prince' (no name given) slaying a dragon in a pit and 'occupying himself with the roasting'.[4] Widespread use of tapestries and embroidered pictures was one important way in which mythological and heroic traditions might travel from one country to another.

As well as the Christian monuments from the Isle of Man showing such scenes, those from Malew, Andreas, Jurby and Ramsey, and the cross still standing in the churchyard at Halton in Lancashire, further examples have been found by James Lang across the Pennines.[5] A slab from a Viking Age cemetery in York shows a man with his thumb in his mouth beside a spit on which meat is roasting, and another fragment from Ripon has a seated figure with his hand to his mouth standing beside what could be parts of a dragon; another figure with hand to mouth is shown beside a headless body at Kirby Hill. Some examples from Scandinavia show that it was possible to use part of the sequence as a kind of shorthand, two favourite motifs being a sword piercing a coiled serpent, and slices of heart on a stick.

The reason for the popularity of the story in Christian art is far from clear. It has been suggested that powerful Scandinavians settled in England and Man wanted to emphasise their descent from the Volsungs, from whom kings traced their ancestry. Another suggestion is that the subject linked pagan and Christian tradition. Jim Lang gives an example from Nunbornholme where a priest is shown holding a chalice, and beneath him two cruder figures seem to have been added, one with his thumb to his mouth and the other with an enormous head, who might represent Sigurd and Regin.[6] This could be seen as the use of the incident where the dragon's blood touches the tongue to remind Christians of the efficacy of the wafer in the Mass. Yet another possibility is that the popular motif of David slaying the lion was replaced in Scandinavian areas by the native one of the hero slaying the dragon. None of these explanations is entirely convincing, but certainly the roasting of the heart and the thumb in the mouth formed an essential part of the tradition by the end of the tenth century and were widely known episodes in a dragon-slaying tale.

The Irish story of the hero placing his thumb in his mouth is told of the young hero Finn mac Cumaill. Like Sigurd, Finn was a warrior leader, and he was followed by bands of fighting men living like outlaws in the forest. Finn was also renowned, however, as a poet and seer, and throughout his life he could receive inspiration by placing his thumb on his 'tooth of knowledge'. The story of how he received this gift bears a marked resemblence to that of Sigurd roasting the dragon's heart.

As a boy, Finn was called Demne, while Finn was the name of his teacher, a poet living beside the River Boyne. Finn the poet wished to eat the flesh of a certain salmon in the river, since he knew that this would bring him such wisdom that nothing would remain unknown to him. He finally caught the salmon and gave it to his pupil to cook for him, and when Demne brought it to him, asked if he had eaten any of it. The boy replied that he had not, 'but I burned my thumb and put it in my mouth'. Thereupon his teacher accepted the fact that the inspiration was meant for Demne, and bestowed his own name upon the boy, telling him: 'It was for you that the salmon was brought to be eaten and you are truly the Finn'. The youth then ate the salmon, and the tale goes on: 'This is what gave knowledge to Finn, for whenever he would put his thumb in his mouth and sing through *teinm laida* [chewing of the pith?], that which he did not know would be revealed to him'.[7]

Another tale, thought by Murphy to be as early as the eighth century,[8] tells how a man from the *Sid* or fairy mound kept stealing food from Finn's men and could not be caught. At last Finn kept watch for him and pursued him, seizing hold of the man as he was entering the mound:[9]

> As Finn stretched his hand towards Culdub, a woman from the *Sid*, with a vessel still moist after the distribution [of drink] in her hand, confronted Finn; she closed the door to the *Sid* so that Finn's finger was squeezed in between the door valve and the doorpost.

Then Finn began to chant, for great knowledge enlightened him from that moment, and he knew the name of the man he had chased into the mound. In one version of the tale it is said that he could afterwards acquire knowledge if he put into his mouth as much of his finger as went into the *Sid*. Nagy suggests that the figure trapped in the door was positioned between two worlds and was thus a symbol of 'inbetweenness', bringing inspiration. A number of tales recorded at various dates contain an incident in which Finn puts either a finger or thumb (usually the latter) into his mouth when he has a problem to solve. Sometimes there is mention of his 'tooth of knowledge', as when in the *Colloquy of the Ancients* we are told: 'He put his thumb under his tooth of knowledge and the truth was revealed to him and falsehood was concealed from him'.[10]

On that occasion Finn's hounds had been stolen and he wanted to discover the thief. On another, a headless body was discovered, and Finn's men asked him whose it was. After using his thumb, Finn recited a poem, which gives a list of the various ways in which the man has not died, as though in reply to a series of questions, and finally revealed the dead man's name.[11] In another tale, Finn and his men were trapped in an Otherworld house, and they begged him to put his thumb under his tooth of knowledge:[12]

> . . . to find out what kind of trouble they were in, what could save them, and whether this was the end of their lives. 'I will', said Finn, 'for a man should do his best when he is in dire straits.' He then put his thumb under the tooth of knowledge so that the truth was revealed to him about the trap that had been prepared for them and how they could be rescued from it, and Finn groaned mournfully.

They asked him if it was the pain in his finger which made him groan, but he denied this, and said he had groaned because the King of Lochlan had trapped them after years of planning and intended to kill them. Nevertheless his special knowledge enabled him to find a way out of their predicament.

The passage implies that Finn was actually biting his thumb, and a similar idea is found in some late folktales. One collected in West Kerry in the nineteenth century tells of the cooking of the salmon:[13]

> He burned his thumb, and to ease the pain put it between his teeth and gnawed the skin to the flesh, the flesh to the bone, the bone to the marrow; and when he had tasted the marrow, he received the knowledge of all things.

An account of the divination rite known as *imbas forosnai* given in Cormac's *Glossary* instructs the seer to chew a piece of red (uncooked) flesh of a pig, dog or cat and place it on a flagstone behind the door, singing an invocation over it.[14] This might possibly be a confused memory of some kind of sacrifice for the acquisition of wisdom, the idea of Finn's finger being crushed being connected with this. Ó hÓgáin points out that confusion between *mér* finger, meaning also a small piece of meat, and *mír* as used in the passage to mean a portion of meat, might have helped to make the directions so difficult to understand.[15]

The use of the thumb to gain wisdom and poetic inspiration is found again in the tale of the young Taliesin, preserved in fairly late manuscripts from the sixteenth century onwards.[16] Taliesin was a Welsh poet of the sixth century (p.53 above), here depicted as a young hero in the world of magic like Sigurd and Finn. He was trained by the witch Ceridwen, who set him to tend a fire under a cauldron, the contents of which were intended to reveal hidden knowledge to her son Morfran. After the cauldron had been heated for a year and a day, three drops of burning liquid out of it fell on the finger of the young man, who at this point had not yet received the name of Taliesin but was called Gwion. He put his finger into his mouth, according to one version of the tale, and like Sigurd immediately realised his danger. The cauldron burst and he fled from the witch, who pursued him, both taking on various shapes; finally Gwion became a grain of wheat and Ceridwen a black hen which gobbled him up. This is the motif of the transformation chase, well known in folktales,[17] but it does not end here with the death of the magician, as is usual. In nine months' time Ceridwen gave birth to Gwion, but he was so beautiful a child that she could not kill him, but instead put him into a bag and threw him into the sea. He was washed ashore near Aberystwyth, where he was rescued and brought up under the name Taliesin, to become a great poet.

Several recognised folktale motifs can be realised in these various tales, not only the Transformation Flight and Conflict, but also the White Snake motif.[18] This is recognisable in the Sigurd tale, where Fafnir seems to be depicted as a serpent rather than a fiery dragon. A characteristic shared by Norse, Irish and Welsh tales is that the hero eats something not intended for him: the dragon's heart was meant for Regin, the salmon for Demne's teacher, and the contents of the cauldron for the witch's son. A further example of this motif is found in the twelfth-century history of Saxo Grammaticus, the Danish scholar writing in Latin of the early traditions of Denmark. He tells in his fifth book of Erik the Eloquent, a hero famed for his courage and his witty and eloquent tongue.[19] He was being brought up by a fostermother called Kraka, along with her own son, and one day she prepared a dish over which she hung snakes of various colours, so that liquid from their jaws dropped into it. She placed the dish with the dark meat opposite her son, but the astute Erik turned it round so that he could help himself to the dark portion, which had a stronger flavour than the rest. The result was that he obtained the gift of wisdom, understood the language of wild beasts and cattle, and became famous for brilliant oratory and quick wit. This idea that wisdom can be acquired through something eaten is found in many later folktales. In Scotland the tale of the roasting of the salmon is told of Paracelsus, and also of a drover called Farquhar Leigh, thought to be Ferchard Leigh, physician to one of the early Scottish kings, as well as of the physicist, Sir James Ramsey.[20] Among local legends collected by Affleck Gray and published in 1987 is one of the wizard Michael Scott, said to live near Selkirk in the thirteenth century.[21] He slew a 'huge white worm', and was offered free lodging at an inn if he would allow the landlord's wife to take the middle portion of the serpent to make into broth. Curious to know how it tasted, Michael rubbed his finger in the spoon used for stirring and sucked it. He immediately received great power and knowledge and understanding of the speech of birds and beasts, and then fled for his life from the wicked innkeeper.

It would probably be a mistake to assume that this well-known tale originated in some crude memory of magic food. The power of understanding the language of birds was taken seriously in Norse tradition, since the ability to interpret bird calls and behaviour was an important skill for warrior leaders, warning of approaching danger. There was also a close link between birds and valkyries, who might take the form of crows and ravens on the battlefield, so that knowledge of bird speech might mean initiation of the hero into the world of Odin and the battle goddesses. Again in early Irish literature the female spirits of battle often appeared in bird form. Roasted meat and the cauldron used for preparing food and drink were also appropriate symbols of hidden knowledge, associated with divination, since they played an important part in the sacrificial feast in honour of the gods. They are ancient mythological symbols, standing for feasting in the Other World and the mead of the gods giving undying youth and wisdom.

Thus one might expect to find some mythological basis behind the tales, although there is no known parallel to the use of the thumb by Finn in the Irish sources, or of Sigurd's touching of his tongue with his thumb in the Icelandic ones. The nearest to the Sigurd episode is that of the eating of the heart of a fierce beast to gain strength and courage.[22] The use of the thumb is not much emphasised in folklore, but the German *Handwörterbuch des deutschen Aberglaubens* (Berlin-Leipzig, 1929–30) has some interesting material under *Daumen*. It seems that the thumb was thought to be particularly sensitive to the supernatural. A man was said to become invisible if he wore a little cap of black fur from the skin of a cat with no white hairs on his left thumb. To capture a demon one had to seize him by his thumb, and to turn the thumb inwards against the palm was a protection against evil spirits in sleep, and also a safeguard against an attack by dogs. This might also absolve one when breaking an oath, with which we may compare the familiar practice among children of crossing the fingers when telling an untruth. Other practices among school children in the mid-twentieth century have been recorded by the Opies, and may be compared with the German material.[23] To turn the thumb into the hand is felt to give strength and protection, and according to a boy from Brixton, will ensure a good examination result. A boy from Romford used the 'Lucky Walls' sign, putting thumbs together to form the letter W with the hands, if about to attempt something difficult; the firm of Walls used this as part of a campaign advertising their ice cream in 1953. The custom of licking a thumb and holding it up when making a bet is still familiar among children in Scotland, and two children agreeing on a wager might lick thumbs and press them together. This practice was known among adults in earlier times, and the Opies give several references; it seems to have been thought legally binding, indicated by such phrases as 'The parties had linked thumbs at finishing a bargain', while in Chambers' *Book of Days* a Scottish lieutenant is stated to have licked his thumb when agreeing to fight a duel in which he lost his life. In Tudor times there are references to raising the thumb to request a truce, and this practice is still found in children's games in Scotland. Children might also link thumbs for luck, or to claim a wish if two of them accidentally said the same word at the same time, an alternative to the linking of little fingers.

Jacob Grimm recorded that men lucky in gaming were said to have the game 'running on their thumbs'. He also mentioned that in the Netherlands the space between thumb and finger was called *Woedenspanne*, a link with the Germanic god Wodan.[24] In this connection it may be noted that on some of the Scandinavian bracteates of the fifth and sixth centuries, based on medallions showing the head of the Roman Emperor with hand upraised (Kendrick's 'Helmet and Hand' style[25]), the hand is so far back that the thumb is practically in the mouth, in a position resembling that on the Sigurd carvings (Fig. 3). Hauck claims a close connection between such figures and the Germanic Wodan.[26] Evidently the hand close to the mouth with the thumb outstretched was familiar in Scandinavia from an early period, although how far this gesture signified power or inspiration is not known.

William Sorrell has made a study of gestures made with the hands, and suggests that the enclosing of the thumb in the hands, characteristic of new-born babies, indicates avoidance of responsibility, whereas to hold the thumb out at a right angle with the fingers indicates a strong personality, which he illustrates by a photograph of a famous conductor

Fig. 3. Gold bracteate from Lellinge, Denmark (from *Die Goldbrakteaten der Völkerwanderungszeit, Munstersche Mittelalterschriften*, 24, 1, 3 1985, taf. 105).

leading an orchestra.[27] This is the position shown on the Viking carvings, and it may be significant that the young hero in the tales considered above is in each case discovering his identity and embarking on his career; in Finn's case, he is acquiring his true name. Desmond Morris in his study of body gestures refers to the thumb as the 'brutal' or 'power' digit. According to him, the placing of the thumb in the mouth does not possess any sexual significance; he and his team have recorded many obscene hand gestures, but this is not one of them.[28] Indeed the fact that it appears on so many Christian monuments of the tenth and eleventh centuries makes it improbable that it had any such significance then either.

In Shakespeare's play *Macbeth* (Act IV, scene 1), one of the witches knows that Macbeth is approaching by the feeling in her thumbs:

> By the pricking of my thumbs
> Something wicked this way comes.
> Open locks, whoever knocks.

Familiar though these lines are, the commentaries give little help as to their interpretation. There is presumably a link with the sensitivity of the thumb as indicated by German folk tradition. A skilled exorcist who entered a house in Cambridge told the owners that he was aware of an overwhelming sense of evil on doing so, recognised by the feeling in his thumbs.[29] A member of the audience to whom this paper was first given told me that she had experienced a pricking sensation in her thumbs when in contact with a colleague with whom she had a difficult relationship.[30] There seem to be some grounds for the suggestion that the thumb was once deliberately used as part of the technique of the seer.

We are left with the problem of the origin of the motif. The earliest carvings in England and the Isle of Man are of tenth-century date, and those in Scandinavia slightly later. It has been claimed that the motif originated in Scandinavia and was later transferred to Ireland,[31] but this I feel to be unlikely. The traditional Scandinavian theme was for the hero to eat the heart of a slain beast in order to gain courage, while it seems that wisdom might be acquired by eating the flesh of a serpent, and both these elements are present in the Sigurd story. Neither Sigurd nor his father Sigmund, the celebrated dragon-slayers, were ever presented as seers. Finn on the other hand was renowned as seer and poet, and a number of different tales of various dates represent him as sucking or biting his thumb in order to obtain knowledge. Although no source known to be early has been found referring to the roasting of the salmon, there is an important carving from Drumhallagh in Donegal which shows two seated men with their thumbs in their mouths facing one another above the arms of a cross. Below the arms are two standing figures, one an ecclesiastic with a crozier and the other a cloaked man with a sword or staff (Fig. 4). In his paper of 1986, Peter Harbison gives a ninth-century date to this cross;[32] this, however, depends on the dubious identification of the standing figures as St Paul and St Anthony, and a number of other scholars would put it much earlier, and see it as work of the eighth or even the seventh century.[33] Murphy interpreted the seated figures as a double picture of Finn foretelling the Crucifixion of Christ,[34] while Françoise Henry suggested that they were weeping angels.[35] A possible alternative could be that they represent early Irish seers who foresaw the coming of Christianity to Ireland. There certainly seem to be good grounds for assuming that this carving belongs to a period well before that of the earliest Sigurd carvings. Like these it is found in a Christian setting; the idea of the seer is in accord with Biblical tradition and would not meet with disapproval from the Church.

Fig. 4. Upright slab, Drumhallagh, Co. Donegal, 1.20 m high (drawing by Eileen Aldworth).

The earliest Sigurd stones are from the Isle of Man and north-western England, areas of Scandinavian settlement in close contact with the Vikings in Ireland. Tales of the thumb in the mouth resulting in the acquisition of knowledge have been found in many parts of the Celtic West, in both Wales and Scotland. There has been much debate as to the direction in which the influence has moved, and presumably the Finn and Sigurd traditions continued to influence one another, while the pictures on crosses and gravestones kept the stories alive. A recent suggestion by Daithi Ó hÓgáin is that the motif developed in Scandinavia out of the Germanic tradition of Sigurd/Siegfried bathing in the dragon's blood to make himself invulnerable to weapons, and perhaps discovering this possibility when he dipped his finger in the blood and found it coated with horn.[36] However, there is no cauldron for boiling meat in any of the early carvings, and the hero is always shown roasting slices of the dragon's heart on a stick over a fire. If the idea of the mantic inspiration by way of the mouth was already familiar to the Scandinavians, and perhaps also the special sensitivity of the thumb, then it is conceivable that the tale of Finn and the salmon would make sense to the Vikings if they encountered it in Ireland, and saw the Drumhallagh carvings or similar ones with the same motif. The position of the hand on some early bracteates certainly suggests that the thumb raised to the mouth had particular significance before the Viking Age. The puzzle remains a tantalising one; whatever the reason for the surprising popularity of the man with his thumb in his mouth in the early middle ages, it clearly possessed special significance for those who made use of the motif in literature and art, and it seems likely that this is due to the familiarity of traditions associated with the seer.

NOTES

1. I have discussed this in greater detail in *Myths and Symbols in Pagan Europe* (Manchester, 1988), 134ff.

2. The word *fingr* in the poem *Fáfnismál* and *Völsunga Saga* can mean either a finger or a thumb.

3. R. N. Bailey, *Viking Age Sculpture* (London, 1980) 116ff.

4. H. R. Ellis, 'Sigurd in the Art of the Viking Age', *Antiquity* 1942, 226ff.

5. J. T. Lang, 'Sigurd and Weland in pre-Conquest carving', *Yorks.Arch.Journ.* 133 (1976), 83ff.

6. *Ibid.*, 89.

7. J. F. Nagy, *The Wisdom of the Outlaw* (California UP, 1985), 214 (from *Macgnimartha Find*, ed. K. Meyer, *Rev.Celt.* 5, 1882, 195–204).

8. G. Murphy, *Duanaire Finn* (Dublin, 1953), lvff.

9. Nagy (note 7), 129–30 (from *Senchas Mór*, ed. K. Meyer, *Rev.Celt.* 25, 1904, 344).

10. Nagy (note 7), 21–2 (from *Agallamn na Seanorach*, ed. N. Ní Shéaghdha, 1942, I,18).

11. Nagy (note 7), 23 (from Cormac's *Glossary in Three Irish Glossaries*, ed. W. Stokes, 1862, xlvi).

12. Nagy (note 7), 23–4 (from *Bruidhean Chaorthainn*, ed. P. Mac Píarais, 1908, 15–16).

13. J. Curtin, *Myths and Folklore of Ireland* (Boston, 1890), 211.

14. *Sanas Cormaic* (ed. O. Bergin *et al*, Halle, 1912), § 756). Cf. N. Chadwick, 'Imbas Forosnai', *Scot.Gael.Stud.* 4 (1935), 97ff; Nagy (note 7), 25–7.

15. D. Ó hÓgáin, 'Magic Attributes of the Hero in Fenian Lore', *The Heroic Process*, ed. B. Almqvist *et al* (Dublin, 1987), 223, note 74.

16. J. Wood, 'The Folklore Background of the Gwion Bach Section of *Hanes Taliesin*', *Bull.Board.Celt.Stud.* 29 (1980–2), 621–34.

17. Stith-Thompson Motif Index: D 615; D 671.

18. Wood (note 16), 621.

19. Saxo Grammaticus, *History of the Danes* V.129 (Fisher and Davidson, 1979–80, I, 124).

20. Wood (note 16), 622ff; R. D. Scott, *The Thumb of Knowledge in Legends of Finn, Sigurd and Taliesin* (New York, 1930), 171ff.

21. A. Gray, *Legends of the Cairngorms* (Edinburgh, 1987), 16–17.

22. E.g. *Hrólfs saga kraka*, 23.

23, I. and P. Opie, *Lore and Language of Schoolchildren* (Oxford, 1959), 227, 231, 129–30.

24. J. Grimm, *Teutonic Mythology* (trans.Stallybrass, 4th ed. [1883], New York, 1966), I, 159–60.

25. T. D. Kendrick, *Anglo-Saxon Art* (London, 1938) 75ff; fig. 14.

26. K. Hauck, *Goldbrakteaten aus Sievern* (Munich, 1970), 187ff.

27. W. Sorrell, *The Story of the Human Hand* (London, 1967), 149.

28. D. Morris *et al*, *Gestures, their Origin and Distribution* (1979); *Manwatching* (London, 1978), 66.

29. Communication from Dr Hilary Belcher.

30. Communication from Miss Beatrice Lewis.

31. A review of various theories is given by R. D. Scott (note 20 above), 212ff; cf. Ó hÓgáin (note 15), 226, note 83.

32. P. Harbison, 'A Group of Early Christian Carved Stone Monuments in County Donegal', *Early Medieval Sculpture in Britain and Ireland* (BAR, British Ser. 152, 1986), 63ff. I am grateful to Isobel Henderson for this reference.

33. F. Henry, *Irish Art in the Early Christian Period* (rev.ed.London, 1965) 123–5 puts this cross in the period before 800; the arguments of U. Roth on dating of Celtic ornament, 'Studien zur Ornamentik frühchristlicher Handschriften des insularen Bereichs' (*Ber.Röm-Germ.Komm.* 60, 1979, 5–214) would make this group of crosses even earlier, and I am grateful to Carola Hicks for this reference. There are, however, differences of opinion as to the dating, and R. B. K. Stevenson (*Journ.Roy.Soc.Antiq.Ireland* 86 (1), 1956, 84–96) argued for a much later date for the series.

34. Murphy (note 8), *lxii*.

35. Henry (note 33), 148, 155.

36. Ó hÓgáin (note 15), 226, note 83.

II. COMPARATIVE STUDIES OF THE SEER

The association of inspiration and knowledge of whatever kind acquired by supernatural means is ancient and widespread. Inspiration, in fact, relates to revealed knowledge. Revelation covers the whole field of human consciousness. It includes knowledge of the past and the hidden present, as well as the future.

N. K. Chadwick, *Poetry and Prophecy* (1946)

6

Dead Reckoning: the Church Porch Watch in British Society

Samuel Pyeatt Menefee

Rev. Sir, At the request of my good friend Mr Saunders, I send you here an account of those things which I heard and saw in *Yorkshire*, whereof he saith he gave you some account when you were at Iroton.

I suppose you may have heard of *watching the Church-yard on St Mark's Eve*. It was frequently practised by those poor ignorant souls where I was. I have heard the manner of it from severall of them. They go two of them on St Mark's Eve, and stand in the Church-yard, within sight of the Church porch and at a certain time of night (they say) the likenes of all those of the parish that shall dye that year, passeth by them into the Church, and in that order they will dye, and when they are all in they hear a murmuring noise in Church for awhile, and then they have power to return. This they tell me was practised at *Pattrington*, and they that watched saw 140 pass into the Church, and one saw the likeness of the other. That year the *plague* came into the town, and so many dyed, and both the persons that watched.

One of my hearers of *Kelnsey* (which you will find in the map) told me a servant of his being in the field at work, a mile from the town, he went down to him, and while he was with him the bel rang. Saith the master, Somebody is dead. Saith the man, it is such an one. Saith the master, how do you know. Saith the man, I was coming over the Church garth one night late, and when I was hard by the Church door, I had no power to stir; by and by there passed by me the likenes of twelve, and this is such an one. I know he is dead, for it is his turn now. And as the man said so it proved. They told me that Easington Church-yard had been often watched, and that it was so one year that I lived there, and the watchers confidently reported that an old woman who was wont to hear me would dye that yer, but they or the devil were mistaken, for she lived more than another. Sr., I fer I shall tire you with reading wt. I am weary with writing . . . I am, Sir, Your reall friend and unworthy Br. in the Lordwork. — Edm. Spencer.

Leicester, July 26, 1673.[1]

I. Introduction

The above letter, written to the nonconformist divine, Richard Baxter,[2] illustrates a practice found throughout England, but particularly in the northern counties: the church porch watch. This ceremony involved a

80

vigil on one of the spirit nights in order to see the shades of those destined to die during the coming year.[3] It was indeed a form of 'dead reckoning'. That title is also appropriate for what will be attempted here, a tally of facts concerning this vanished British custom and an attempt to chart a course to arrive at a better understanding of this institution. In evaluating the church porch watch and its place in British society, attention will be paid to the belief's form and practitioners, the symbolism involved, the results experienced by those who watched in the church porch, and the web of popular tradition which surrounded the practice.

II. 'I Have Heard the Manner of It': The Form of the Belief

John Aubrey, in his *Remains of Gentilism and Judaism*, noted:

> It was a Custome for some people that were more curious than ordinary, to sitt all night in the Church porch of their Parish on midsomer-eve, that is, St John Baptist's eve; and they should see, the apparitions of those that should die in the parish that yer come and knock at the dore . . .[4]

He commented: 'the Civill warres comeing on have putt all these Rites, or customes quite out of fashion. Warres not only extinguish Religion and Lawes: but Superstition: and no suffimen is a greater fugator of Phantosmes, than Gun-powder'.[5] The Church Porch Watch, however, was practised from at least the late seventeenth century until almost the end of Victoria's reign.[6] Found in northern and western England and in Wales,[7] the belief involved a vigil on some major calendrical night — St Mark's Eve (April 24 — apparently preferred), New Year's Eve, Midsummer Eve, Halloween, or Christmas Eve.[8] Usually, this required a watch in the church or churchyard, although in Wales, *hearing*, not sight, was primary.[9] The vigil might take place between eleven and one, or the spirits might appear exactly at midnight.[10] According to some, those doomed to die would not be seen until the *third* such watch. Fasting might be necessary prior to the vigil;[11] it was also claimed that those who watched *once* would be forced to continue until that eve when they saw their *own* spirits in the procession, while those who dozed were doomed to death within the year.[12] A would-be participant might station himself in a number of locations: in church, directly outside, or in the church porch.[13] He or she might watch in the churchyard, or from the safety of the lych gate.[14] Even more removed were other vantage points — a nearby lane, a crossroad, or a window look-out.[15] Occasionally, physical action was necessary. Near Kendall, a watcher needed to circle the church *backwards* three times before taking a seat in the porch, while Winterton belief required one to walk around the church eleven times, sticking a pin in each window.[16] In Northamptonshire, a 'dare ceremony' was grafted onto the vigil:[17]

> [T]hey go in the evening and lay in the church porch a branch of a tree or a flower, large enough to be readily found in the dark, and then return home to wait the approach of midnight. They are to proceed to the porch again before the clock strikes twelve, and to remain in it till it has struck; as many as choose accompanying the maid who took the flower or branch . . . as far as the church gate, and there wait until their adventuring companion returns.[18]

Having found an observation point, it only remained to await the spirits. These arrived and performed in different ways. Aubrey reported that the wraiths of those to die came and knocked on the church door,[19] while others said that those foredoomed actually entered the building.[20] One version holds that:

> those that come to an untimely end, are represented by their ghostly proxies, in the very article of dissolution. If a person is to be hanged, or to hang himself, as Burns says in his 'Tam O'Shanter', 'Wi' his last gasp his gab will gape'. If the person is to be drowned, his representative will come as if struggling and splashing in water, and so on in other cases of premature death.[21]

In many instances, the tableau unfolded in the order in which the deaths were to occur over the ensuing twelvemonth.[22] This assembly was apparently for a 'Service of the Dead'.[23] According to one Winterton resident, 'you will see in a vision the coffins carried into the church containing the bodies of all who are to die within the year'.[24] The poet John Clare speaks of 'a coffin covered with a white sheet [seeming] to be born by shadows without heads'.[25] This corresponds with Powell's report from Wiltshire that '[m]en without heads have been seen in the church, and a little child, and "a terr'ble sight of galleysome [fearful] things"'.[26] Old Peggy Richard of Northorpe thus described her vision of the 'risen dead' on St Mark's Eve: 'They walked about the churchyard with the flesh rotting from their bones'.[27] Alternatively, the 'unchancyness' of the sights might be related to their method of locomotion: 'Infants and young children, not yet able to walk, are said to roll in on the pavement'.[28] Several accounts emphasise that the spirits are 'dhrissed i' ther natt'reel cleeas'[29] — a foredoomed rector was in fact recognised by his surplice, and was later buried where his spirit had 'vanished' in the churchyard.[30] This is itself a sample of a variant of the belief — 'that the ghosts of those who were to die came *out* of the church, walked round the churchyard and, having found the site of their future graves, lay down and vanished underground'.[31] Tyack reports a formal churchyard procession in which 'the wraiths of the doomed walk[ed] . . . in solemn state around the churchyard, preceded by the parish clerk'.[32] Most say that the unlucky watcher would eventually see *himself*, but one source holds that individuals were *incapable* of glimpsing their own wraiths.[33]

Occasionally, marriage as well as death was foretold. Kendal watchers might see the 'ghosts' of intended husbands or wives pass before them, multiple apparitions if they were to be wedded more than once.[34] John Clare states that lucky female participants could see 'their own persons hanging on [the] arms of their future husbands with the priest &c as if going [to] be married & as many couples as bridemen & Maidens as they shall see following them so many months shall it be ere they are married . . .'[35] Others report that *all* the local spirits go to church — those who are to die within the year not returning, those who will suffer sickness exiting the building after a delay, couples to be married appearing arm-in-arm, and maidens and bachelors returning singly.[36] Those Welsh versions which place the emphasis on sound, not sight, hold that 'the spirits', 'a ghostly voice', or the Devil himself reads or calls out the names of those doomed to die within the year.[37]

III. 'A Terror to the Neighborhood': Participants in the Church Porch Watch

Who were the practitioners of this dread ceremony? Katherine Foxegale of Walesby, Nottinghamshire, was presented before the ecclesiastical court in 1608 for this practice and for being 'a daylie scolde & curser of her neighbours'.[38] About 1630, Robert Hallywell, a tailor, and Edward Vicars, curate to Mr William Dalby, attempted this ritual at Axholme, Lincolnshire. The resulting revelations caused quite a stir: 'The lord Sheffield . . . sent for Hallywell to receive account of . . . [the ceremony]. The fellow fearing my Lord would cause him to watch the church porch againe, he hid himself in the Carrs till he was almost starved'.[39] Finally there is the servant at Kelnsey, Yorkshire, who proved accurate in predicting 'for whom the bell tolled'.[40]

Information on practitioners in the early years of the next century is scanty. According to Baring-Gould, Peter Priestly, sexton of the church of All Saints at Wakefield, Yorkshire, attempted the ritual to determine the briskness of his trade in the coming year — with comic results.[41] From the later eighteenth century, 'Joe Brown' was said to watch the churchyard in the West Riding of Yorkshire. 'This man', says a source who was a boy at the time:

> used to inspire my youthful fancy with great awe. I was not the only one who regarded him with fear: he contrived by a certain mysterious behaviour, to impress weak and youthful minds with feelings which bordered upon terror. His person is

vividly imprinted on my memory; his face was broad, his features coarse, and he had what is called a hare-lip, which caused him to speak through the nose, or *snaffle*, as they term it in Yorkshire. He never would directly acknowledge that he watched the church; but a mysterious shrug or nod tended to convey the assertion. Two circumstances which took place in my remembrance, served to stamp his fame as a ghost-seer. At the fair-tide he quarreled with a young man, who put him out of the room in which they were drinking; he told his antagonist that he would be under the sod before that day twelve months, which happened to be the case. The other circumstance was this; he reported a young man would be drowned, who lived in the same street in which my father's house was situated. I well remember the report being current early in the year. On Easter Sunday, a fine young man, a bricklayer's apprentice, went to bathe in the river Ouse, (which runs by C--d [Cawood], my native town) and drowned; this fulfilled his prediction, and made him to be regarded with wonder.[42]

Subsequently, 'Joe Brown' joined one religious sect. When expelled for 'mal-practices', he soon joined another.[43] Associating himself with a 'loose young man' (who was eventually transported),[44] '[t]hey commenced a system of petty plunder, which soon increased to more daring acts of robbery and burglary'.[45] Here, too, supernatural belief played a role. Dressed as a 'Barguest', a goblin whose appearance foretold death or a great calamity, Joe chased away the superstitious, leaving the way open for him and his companion to plunder the abandoned premises![46] Pressed by a warrant relating to a local burglary, the two left the Cawood area for a time:[47]

> They went to a small town where they were not known and assumed the disguise of fortune-tellers. 'Old Joe' was the 'wise man', and affected to be dumb, whilst his younger confederate . . . interpreted his mystic signs. They lodged at a house kept by two aged sisters, spinsters. They found that these females were possessed of a little money, and kept it in a box. One night they gave their hostesses sweetened ale, in which they had infused a quantity of laudanum. One of the poor women never woke again, but the other lived. These men were taken up and examined, but liberated for want of proof. They afterwards were suspected of having shot the Leeds and Selby carrier in the night; at length they were taken for stealing some hams, and in consequence of their bad character, sentenced to transportation for life . . . When about to be embarked for Botany Bay, Joe, either touched by conscience, or through reluctance to leave England, made a confession of his crimes. He and his companion were removed from the Isle of Wight to York castle. Joe alone was put on his trial, and, though not convicted on his own confession, corroborating circumstances of his guilt were produced, and the sister of the poisoned female appeared against him. He was found guilty of the murder, and executed at York, at the Lent assizes of 1809.[48]

In the nineteenth century, according to John Nicholson's *Folk Lore of East Yorkshire*: 'Fortune-tellers went, or acquired the reputation of going, thus to watch, so that their patrons might be informed if they were to die soon. Doubtless, a liberal fee procured the desired information'.[49]

One such was Margaret Dove, known locally as 'Old Peg Doo', who 'used to watch on St Mark's Eve, in the north porch of the Priory Church, Bridlington'. 'The divulging of the information thus obtained formed a considerable income, for the fearful ones were glad to pay for the pleasure of knowing they had to live another year, and the fated ones had time to set their affairs in order.'[50] S.G. of Driffield flourished circa 1815:

> [She] was famous all over the country side as a wise woman and fortune teller. Very, very numerous are the people who have gone to her to have their enterprise foretold, or to consult her as to the wisdom of certain intended speculations. Maidens went to know if their love-affairs would prosper; anxious ones went to enquire if their forms had entered the church porch, which was only a short distance in front of the wise woman's house, and there she watched on St Mark's Eve; tradesmen might be seen there after dark, to know if their business would improve under certain alterations; and fearful mothers enquired if their absent children were well and prosperous . . . and if the fates were propitious they might have some vision of the absent one, which sent them away rejoicing.[51]

S.G. was adept at discovering the whereabouts of stolen property. Perhaps not surprisingly she was also tainted with hints of diablerie; local children were afraid to meet her, and when she died she was said to have 'flew ower Driffield chotch . . . on a blazin' besom'.[52] In a similar manner, 'Milkey Lawrence' of Flamborough, who also watched on St Mark's Eve, was believed to bring bad luck to those fishermen who met her on their way to sea.[53] The 'wizard of Redmire' in the North Riding could 'foretell weeks and months in advance the death of any inhabitant'. He remained silent, however, when the porch watch produced any of his friends: '[A]t such times his wife obtained the secret by his disturbed dreams and unearthly groans during sleep.' It is said that 'a sigh of relief passed through the village' at the wizard's death.[54] Nor were such watchers confined to Yorkshire. In John Clare's Northamptonshire village

> an odd character who had no fear calld Ben Barr a prophet usd [to] watch the poach every year & pretended to know [the] fates of every one in the villages round as who shoud be married or dye in the year but as few pence generally predicted a good omen he seldom prophesied the deaths of his believers.[55]

Barr's popularity may itself be divined from the fact that he soon moved on to escape the wrath of the locals.[56]

Another group who watched in the porch were minor church officials. William Henderson reports that one old sexton did so 'to count the gains of the coming year'.[57] The same was true of Jonny Joneson, a sexton known by Samuel Bamford of Middleton.[58] At a meeting of the Wainfleet Men's Guild in 1889, a local mechanic stated that the parish clerk and sexton of Theddlethorpe always 'set out St Mark's Eve, aiming to know how much he'd addle in happin foak up th'yer, an' he were nivver far out in his

reckonin', an' I knaw as it's gospel trewth . . .'[59] Detailed information
has survived on Michael Parker of Malton, who was born in 1758 and
died in 1823.[60] Parker was twice married — his first wife dying, and
his second absconding.[61] Only one of his children survived infancy — a
son who died aged eighteen.[62] Michael hawked coals for a living, but also
served as gravedigger to the parish of Malton.[63] He collected unusual
bones 'and a constant propensity to increase his collections, exposed him
to the suspicion and displeasure of his neighbours'.[64] He was a source of
humour to the local children, and for some unkind adults, as '[h]e had a
stammering, hesitating tone, with a peculiar lisp in certain words, which
was often very amusing to his auditors'.[65] Michael was also the butt of
practical jokes, ranging from 'kidnapping' of his son (when the child was
still alive) to an attempt to force Michael to attend a Methodist meeting (he
was a staunch Anglican), and giving him the (false) news that his second
wife had died.[66]

> As he became old, he sometimes, under provocation, gave utterance to rough
> expressions, foreign to his kindly disposition. More than once he was heard to
> say to his wanton persecutors, that 'he should have them some day, and he would,
> certainly, bury them with their faces downward.' Versed in the superstitions of the
> vulgar, he regularly observed the periodical return of St Mark's eve . . . To one
> of his abusers he said that he had seen him on St Mark's eve, and should have
> him soon. Observations of this nature obtained him enemies, and expressions of
> real sorrow which he often manifested on the indisposition of his neighbours, were
> sometimes regarded as insincere, and his approach to the dwellings of the afflicted
> forbidden.[67]

Related to this grouping are individuals whose jobs and location gave
them opportunity to watch. In Dorset, for example, 'George Cairns,
the toll-keeper at Lyon's Gate, used to watch all midsummer's night to
see *the spirits* go to Buckland Church and come back again'.[68] Similarly
situated was

> Robert Staff, who formerly kept the Maid's Head Inn at Stalham [Norfolk], opposite
> to the church . . .[H]e and two other men . . . watched the church porch, opposite
> to the house, on St Mark's Eve . . .[H]e would never tell anybody who were to die
> or to be married, 'for he did not watch with that intent'.[69]

The location of the inn, of course, is similar to that of S.G.'s house.[70]
Unidentified older men and women sat up for the vigil which, at least
occasionally, made them 'an object of some dread' to their neighbours.[71]
In Somerset, a drunken braggart is said to have waited in Crowcombe
church porch on a bet, while in the Faroe Islands, visions were limited
to those with 'second sight'.[72] Also, *groups* of young men or women
attempted the ritual when their courage allowed.[73] The Luggar brothers
are said to have done this at Travistock church around the beginning of

the nineteenth century — for their temerity, both suffered death within the year; a young carpenter in Monk-Okehampton did the same.[74] Two men in Marrick, Yorkshire, planned to undertake the vigil, 'but they were so afraid of falling asleep that they turned back'.[75]

The prime rationale prompting the bulk of such vigilants was *power*.[76] It is obvious that wise women and wizards would have enhanced their trade by such a recognised link with the supernatural. Semi-professionals, like Ben Barr, seem to have built their practice on this. Even in the case of a local with no other supernatural pretences, it was noted that '[t]he villagers always came to him in case of sickness in their family, to ask if the afflicted would recover'.[77] Although there is no evidence that they *profited* from such knowledge, clerks and sextons and those whose houses placed them in a 'physical position' to know would surely have enhanced their standing by undertaking the ritual.[78] In the case of Michael Parker, at least, the 'knowledge' gained by the ritual provided an unanswerable comeback: 'I saw you on St Mark's Eve and I'll have you soon!'.[79] Nor was it uncommon that a person might be taunted by a watcher about impending death. One church watcher in Lincolnshire told an individual that her brother would die, while another informant reported 'that her mother lived more than a year after she was told by a church-watcher (a woman in the next parish), that she would die within the year'.[80] It is reported that '[t]he persons making, or supposed to have made, this vigil, are a terror to the neighbourhood. At the least offense they are apt, by significant looks or hints, to insinuate to the credulous the speedy death of some valued friend or relative'.[81] With such manifestations of power it is easy to see how certain individuals were drawn to the ritual, *whatever* the results.

IV. 'Sit Thee Down/in the Church Porch, and Think What Thou Hast Seen': Symbolism of the Belief

Following Christopher Harvey's exhortation,[82] it is time to consider some of the symbolism surrounding the Church Porch Watch. One obvious candidate for examination is the church porch. This location exemplified the three ages of man; not only were baptismal fonts located here, but the porch was also a place for marriages and burials.[83] Beggars and penitents stood in the porch, seeking worldly or otherworldly salvation.[84] Indeed, this location was a microcosm of the life of the community:

> Several councils and synods issued decrees forbidding the trial of pleas in the church or its porches, and the number of prohibitions is in some measure a proof that such secular uses were not unknown if indeed they were uncommon. Fairs and merchandise

D

from time to time invaded the porches in spite of many protests . . .[N]otices of elections rates, and other worldly matters . . . may still be read on the doors and in the porches of churches.[85]

The 'porch was in former days the place often selected for the payment of dowries, legacies, and other monies' as witnesses for these acts were usually present.[86] 'When the porch was chambered it furnished a place for the sacristan, or for night watchers, who . . . could, by looking into the church, see that it was safe from fire and sacrilege'.[87] Not incidentally, this also provided a place for aspiring church porch watchers.

In addition to representing the ages of man, and society in microcosm, the porch stood as a dividing line between the sanctified church and the everyday world — a boundary between sacred and profane.[88] As William Axon notes in his discussion of the porch, '[t]he separation of the religious from the secular has never been complete'.[89] At least one ballad version of 'The Cruel Mother' uses the porch for a supernatural meeting between a mother and the child she murdered:

> As she was going to the church,
>   She saw a sweet babe in the porch.
> 'O sweet babe, and thou were mine,
>   I wed cleed thee in the silk so fine.'
> 'O mother dear, when I was thine,
>   You did na prove to me sae kind.'[90]

It is thus easy to understand why the church porch was the scene of such vigils. Locations such as the lych gate or an overlooking window also represented boundaries between natural and supernatural, with their added distance from church and graveyard providing the participant an increased margin of safety.[91] The circumambulation of churches as an 'unscrewing' of the supernatural has been dealt with elsewhere;[92] it should be noted, however, that the version of this belief in which a pin was placed at each church window is related to the use of iron to protect the venturing mortal from supernatural influence.[93] Both crossroads and lanes had their own associations.[94]

The times of the vigil are also of symbolical importance. Not only were they used for several forms of divination, but they represented temporal boundaries in the year equivalent to the spatial boundaries of the ritual's locus.[95] Christmas and Midsummer are close to the equinox, while May Eve, traditionally balancing Halloween, is less than a week away from St Mark's Eve. At these 'chinks in time', supernatural influences supposedly invaded the physical world so that it would not have been surprising that a person could glimpse futurity. On these nights spirits were believed to be *particularly* active.[96] In a similar manner, midnight, a boundary between days, was another propitious time for supernatural encounters.[97]

The occasional requirement to make *three* vigils before getting results is related to the symbolic power of that number; it can be compared to the multiple circumambulations of the church.[98] Additionally, this version of the belief would have explained why no results were garnered on *any* watches before the third attempt.[99] Fasting was a common preparation for vigils. Lack of food heightened sensibilities and perhaps helped to produce 'supernatural' visions.[100] The use of the vigil itself is interesting, allowing a participant contact with the supernatural and access to 'hidden' knowledge. Characteristic of many 'primitive' cultures, this method of ascertaining the future was also widespread in Britain and Europe — particularly where love divinations were concerned.[101] Even the element of compulsion in certain texts serves a purpose; its connection with witchcraft and diablerie suggests the *negative* connotations of the watch.[102]

The visions produced were often extremely stylised, giving hints as to the time, sequence, and method of death, or differentiating between that change of state and marriage or sickness. This was in accordance with many summoning divinations which purport to reveal 'the color of his hair/the clothes he will wear', the identity of the destined spouse's trade, or his status in life.[103] Even some of the more outlandish visions may formerly have had a symbolic import; the mourners without heads[104] may be compared to the ghosts of four bridesmaids at Great Melton, Norfolk: 'If you see their pretty faces, all is well; but sometimes they are headless, and this foretells disaster'.[105]

V. 'I Have Heard 'em tell Strange Stories of it': The Web of Tradition

John Aubrey, *in Remaines of Gentilisme and Judaisme*, notes:

> Memorandum: the sitting-up on Midsommer-eve in the Church-porch, to see the Apparitions of those that should dye, or be buried there, that Yeare: mostly used by women: I have heard 'em tell strange stories of it.[106]

And what sorts of stories were these? Research into this tradition yields several motifs which bear similarities to those concerned with other divinations.

A. *Correct prediction of another's death*: Watchers were not always reticent about naming names of those to die.[107] When the person so named conveniently expired,[108] or when someone who might have been seen during a watch met an untimely end, this strengthened popular perception of the ritual's accuracy. According to the *Westmoreland Gazette*:

> When any one sickens that is thought to have been seen in this manner, it is presently whispered about that he will not recover; for that such a one who has watched St Mark's Eve says so. Such fancies oftentimes cause illness and death. Many persons are actually said to have died through the mere impression made upon their minds by such gossip.[109]

It is often difficult to distinguish fact from fiction. The Bridestowe, Devon, man who died at harvest time — possibly of fright although he had had a brief illness — sounds like a real-life casualty.[110] On the other hand the tradition connected to George Cairns, who told one woman: "'You have a fine little girl there, but her spirit did not come back from the church", and she died within a year'[111] appears to be more of a tale. It is paralleled by the story of a man at Corringham, Lincolnshire, who refused to say what he had seen during the hours of his watch: "'I'm not allowed to tell . . . but one thing I'll say, my wife will die within the year". She died suddenly at the end of three months'.[112] Mr March, a former rector of Ford, Northumberland, was seen in his surplice on St Mark's Eve by two casual passers-by: '[t]hat night the rector was taken ill, and died the following day, his grave being dug just where the vision had disappeared'.[113]

B. *Prediction of death in response to complaint*: A characteristic version of this motif heralds from Martin in Timberlake, Lincolnshire: '[M]any years ago there was an old clerk who church watched, and once when a farmer grumbled at the rates he said: "You need not trouble, for you'll not have to pay them", nor had he, for he went home and died within three months of the shock'.[114] Another apparent example comes from Exmoor — 'a tailor was remonstrated with for his tardiness in completing a suit of clothes. He testily replied that there was no necessity for haste, as the customer would be dead within a twelvemonth . . .'[115] This carried an implicit message (that it is unwise to antagonise a church porch watcher) which would have promoted the social prestige of these individuals, and of the ritual itself.

C. *Unusual prediction of death*: Occasionally this takes the form of being able to predict the *order* of death.[116] In other examples, what makes the prediction unusual is the *number* of individuals seen who subsequently die — like the 140 shades at Pattrington, foretelling the plague.[117] The results may prove unusual in other ways; one watcher saw *two* brides, both of whom he later married.[118] Or individuals predicted to die may appear healthy during most of the year, decline swiftly, and still die within the annual deadline.[119] Perhaps the most spectacular versions of such stories relate to deaths which appear unlikely, but which nevertheless occur according to schedule.[120] One such story is given by Gervase Hollis of Great Grimsby, Lincolnshire. This colonel in Charles I's service heard the story from the Rev. Lemewell Rampaine, the local minister, who was household chaplain to Sir Thomas Munson of Burton:[121]

> In the year 1634, two men (inhabitants of Burton) agreed betwixt themselves upon St Mark's eve at night to watch in the churchyard at Burton, to try whether or no (according to the ordinary belief amongst the common people) they should see the Spectra, or Phantasma of those persons which should die in that parish the year following. To this intent, having first performed the usual ceremonies and superstitions, late in the night, the moon shining then very bright, they repaired to the church porch, and there seated themselves, continuing there till near twelve of the clock. About which time (growing weary with expectation and partly with fear) they resolved to depart, but were held fast by a kind of insensible violence, not being able to move a foot. About midnight, upon a sudden (as if the moon had been eclipsed), they were environed with a black darkness; immediately after, a kind of light, as if it had been a resultancy from torches. Then appears coming toward the church porch, the minister of the place, with a book in his hand, and after him one in a winding sheet, whom they both knew to resemble one of their neighbours. The church doors immediately fly open, and through pass the apparitions, and then the doors clap to again. Then they seem to hear a muttering, as if it were the burial service, with a rattling of bones and noise of earth, as in the filling up of a grave. Suddenly a still silence, and immediately after the apparition of the curate again, with another of their neighbours following in a winding-sheet, and so a third, fourth, and fifth, every one attended with the same circumstances as the first. These all having passed away, there ensued a serenity of the sky, the moon shining bright, as at the first; they themselves being restored to their former liberty to walk away, which they did sufficiently affrighted. The next day they kept within doors, and met not together, being both of them exceedingly ill, by reason of the affrightment which had terrified them the night before. Then they conferred their notes, and both of them could very well remember the circumstance of every passage. Three of the apparitions they well knew to resemble three of their neighbours; but the fourth (which seemed an infant), and the fifth (like an old man), they could not conceive any resemblance of. After this they confidently reported to every one what they had done and seen; and in order designed to death those three of their neighbours, which came to pass accordingly.[122]

There still remained, however, the sticky problem of the two unrecognised shades:

> Shortly after . . . the three deaths, a woman in the town was delivered of a child, which died likewise. So that now there wanted but one (the old man), to accomplish their predictions . . . In that winter, about mid-January, began a long and sharp frost, during the continuance of which some of Sir John Munson's friends in Cheshire, having some occasion of intercourse with him, despatched away a foot messenger (an ancient man), with letters to him. This man, travelling this bitter weather over the mountains in Derbyshire, was nearly perished with cold, yet at last he arrived at Burton with his letters, where within a day or two he died. And these men, as soon

as ever they see him, said peremptorily that he was the man whose apparition they see [sic], and that doubtless he would die before he returned, which accordingly he did.[123]

Some two hundred years later this story was *still* current in Lincolnshire in a form collected by Mrs Peacock:

My grandfather used to tell of old S. who lived at Kirton-in-Lindsey. This man was in the habit of watching the church. One year a neighbour said to him, 'You know who is going to die within the year, now just tell us their names'. But he would not satisfy him their curiosity beyond saying, 'There will be a death in the market-place'. One or two were ill during the year, but contrary to expectations they all recovered, and time went on till St Mark's was nearly round again. Then some horse-riders came to the town, and one of them dropped down dead as he was walking across the market place . . .[124]

Such stories would have enhanced credibility for the ritual by suggesting that even an 'obviously wrong' prediction might prove correct when all the facts were in.[125]

D. *Ill fortune follows for church porch watcher*: Robert Hunt reports of the custom that:

This is so serious an affair that it is not, I believe, often tried. I have, however, heard of young women who have made the experiment. But every one of the stories relate that, coming last in the procession, they had seen shadows of themselves; that from that day forward they have pined, and ere midsummer has again come round, that they have been laid to rest in the village graveyard.[126]

Versions of this form of the belief are widespread. A carpenter at Monk-Okehampton fancied he saw himself. 'Vainly did rector and doctor remonstrate with him . . . [D]espite all reassurances he died within two weeks.'[127] The Lugger brothers, also from Devon, saw their own shades in a spectral funeral procession and passed away shortly thereafter.[128] A roadman in Somerset (in 1938) tells of a Crowcombe widower, who watched the porch to see his wife's *ghost*. 'He didn't live after zo long as a bird's twitter, he were drawed away to a shred, and his life was a-took.'[129] Much the same ending applies in northern England. Jonny Joneson, mentioned by Samuel Bamford, saw himself,[130] as did the sexton at Theddlethorpe,[131] and old women at Scarborough and Westerdale.[132] An enquiring Yorkshire man, straining to see the features of the spectral corpse, heard 'a whisper . . . through the quiet midnight air, " 'Tis yourself!" '[133]

In an alternative form, death comes only to one of the group. Richard Bovet, in *Pandaemonium or the Devil's Cloyster* (1684), notes that during the course of one such session, 'one of the watchers . . . fell fast asleep so that none of the company could awaken her, during the time of which profound sleep, the likeness of that party appeared, and knocked at the Church door . . .'[134] Grose too tells a similar story.[135] The classic example, however, is the account by Thomas Codd, rector of Laceby, Lincolnshire:[136]

> At Axholme, alias Haxey in ye Isle, one Mr Edward Vicars (curate to Mr Wm Dalby, vicar) together with one Robert Hallywell a taylor, intending on St Mark's even at night to watch in ye church porch to see who should die in ye year following (to this purpose using divers ceremonies), they addressing themselves to the business, Vicars (being then in his chamber) wished Hallywell to be going before and he would presently follow him. Vicars fell asleep, and Hallywell (attending his coming in ye church porch) forthwith sees certaine shapes presenting themselves to his view, resemblances (as he thought) of divers of his neighbours, who he did nominate, and all of them died the yeare following, and Vicars himselfe (being asleep) his phantom was seen of him also and dyed with ye rest. This sight made Hallywell so agast that he looks like a Ghost ever since. The Lord Sheffield (hearing this relation) sent for Hallywell to receive account of it. The fellow fearing my Lord would cause him to watch the church porch againe he hid himselfe in the Carrs till he was almost starued. The number of those that died (whose phantasmes Hallywell saw) was as I take it about fowerscore.[137]

Bowker, in *Goblin Tales of Lincolnshire*, gives a similar version — a clergyman of Walton-le-Dale, accompanied by a 'herb-doctor', saw his own spirit. He left the parish and died within the year of a fever caught when ministering at a cottage; the 'herb-doctor' would never repeat the experiment.[138]

In other cases the ill fortune varies. A Somerset braggart 'never spoke of what he saw but went so "white as a sheet".'[139] Somerset vigils held other dangers:

> If you watch by the gate at midnight on All Hallow's Night to see who will die within the coming year you are in danger of being the first comer yourself and you will become the 'churchyard walker' and the guardian of the graveyard until another foolhardy and impious person disturbs the Service of the Dead . . . The man or woman who is stealthily touched by the Church-Yard Walker (even his icy breath is fatal) dies then and there or only lives long enough to curse his sacrilegeous curiosity.[140]

Madness might result, as it did for the father who saw his daughter in the spectral procession.[141] In Leicestershire, one watcher saw first his sister, then his mother, then himself in the grisly parade![142] Presumably such stories made many reluctant to try the ritual, helping to preserve it in folk belief as an accurate, but sometimes deadly, ceremony.

All of these four motifs, therefore, tended to reinforce the bona fides of the ceremony, by indicating its accuracy, by building up the prestige of the watchers, or by discouraging individuals from engaging frivolously in the practice.

VI: Second Thoughts on Second Sight: Some Practical Results of the Church Porch Watch

In the discussion of practitioners, mention has already been made of some aspects of the community's reaction to church porch watchers. Two situations, however, remain to be considered for which some evidence exists: the reaction of church authority to the watch, and failed attempts to go through with the ceremony.

One *possible* reference to the ritual comes from the Act book of the Consistory Court of Wells. On April 18, 1584,

> The Official was informed that John Panter of the parish of Dultyng was accustomed to go to *mendepe* [. . . Mendip] on the Eve of St John the Baptist to consult devils . . . and that he had answers from them which he related at length to William Joly of Shepton Mallet and others, and that he was in the habit of doing this each year.[143]

More certain is the July 26, 1608 presentment of Katherine Foxegale of Walesby, 'for a daylie scolde & curser of her neighbours & for watching uppon Sainte Markes even at nighte laste in the Church porche to presage by devilishe demonstracion the deathe of somme neighbours within the yeare'.[144] Even more recently, there is evidence that Somerset churchmen attempted to stop the practice; a gate studded with nails was erected at one church to discourage would-be watchers.[145]

Many attempts at the watch were stillborn. In Cambridgeshire, about 1812, a practical joke was played on certain villagers who went to watch the church at Whittlesford — greeted with (earthly) groans, moans, noises, and the tolling of the church bell, the would-be vigilants fled the scene.[146] Sabine Baring-Gould reports the fears which broke up one Devon watch:

> Shopland . . . told me that he and ten other men had resolved to watch over midnight in the tower of Broadwood Church to see the spirits, or the doubles, go by who would show who were to die within a twelvemonth. But all failed to keep the appointment save two, himself and one other. However, as midnight approached, his companion's courage gave way and he deserted his post. This was too much for Shopland, and he also retreated from the church tower and yard. But as he looked behind him he saw some mysterious white object drawing itself across the roof; he was too frightened to remain and find out what manner of creature this was.[147]

In Yorkshire, in the latter nineteenth century, two young fellows attempted the watch at Marrick 'but they were so afraid of falling asleep [a prediction of impending death] that they turned back'.[148]

Both of these practical situations — ecclesiastical actions against the belief and abortive ceremonies — could have increased belief in the ritual's veracity, and reinforced the web of traditions surrounding the practice.

VII. Conclusion

And where does this 'dead reckoning' lead? It suggests that the Church Porch Watch was a custom of some antiquity in western England, Wales and the North. Practitioners were generally of three sorts: professional or semi-professional seers, minor church officials or those living or working near the church, and young thrill-seekers. In each case, the ritual, though it had negative connotations, provided social status within the community. The ritual's temporal and physical locations marked boundaries between the natural and supernatural, and symbolism played a large role in structuring the belief. At least four tale motifs are associated with the practice: correct prediction of another's death, prediction of death in response to a complaint, unusual predictions which were fulfilled, and the ill-luck which dogged church porch watchers. All of these played a part in supporting the belief, as did persecution by the church and abortive attempts at the practice.

NOTES

(Due to considerations of space, most references are *illustrative* rather than *exhaustive* in nature.)

1. Mrs Gutch, *County Folklore* VI: *E. Riding of Yorkshire* (1912), 44. This letter refers to events c.1666 ('about 17 years agoe') when the writer served as chaplain to Col. Robert Overton of Easington Hall, Holderness.

2. *Ibid.*

3. These include the following motifs:

D 1825.1.2.(j) [Watching at church door or porch . . . on St Mark's Eve to 'see' who will marry].

D 1825.6 [Magic powers to 'see' who will die . . .]

D 1825.6.1. [Watching at the church door . . . Spirits of those to die . . . may enter the church or fail to enter].

D 1825.6.1.(a) [Unrecognised spirits . . . later accounted for].

D 1825.6.1.(a) [Unrecognised spirit, messenger from nearby town . . . another . . . still-born child].

D 1825.6.1.(b) [Watcher . . . must watch each following year].

D 1825.6.2 [Watcher . . . sees his own spirit].

D 1825.6.2.(a) [Watcher not to die if his spirit turns and looks at him . . .].

D 1825.6.2.(b) [Watcher sees his own spirit . . . realises he is to die].

D 1825.6.2.(c) [Watcher . . . goes to sleep and does not see own spirit]. (E. W. Baughman, *Type and Motif Index of the Folk-tales of England and North America*, (Bloomington, Ind., 1966), 118, 119.

4. c.1688. John Aubrey, 'Remaines of Gentilisme and Judaisme', in J. Buchanan-Brown, ed., *John Aubrey, Three Prose Works* (London, 1972), 207.

5. *Ibid.*

6. Late 17th c.: see notes 1, 3 above; Victoria's reign: Rev. R. M. Heanley, 'Paper on the Vikings', *Saga Book Vik. Club* 3 (1902), 43; cf. *Brit Calend Cust* II (1938) 190–91 (belief mentioned as current at Men's Guild Meeting, Wainfleet, Lincs., 1889).

7. Northern: A. R. Wright, T. E. Lones, *Brit. Calend. Cust.* II (1938), 189–92; Western: *Ibid.* III (1940), 19–20; Wales, T. Gwyn Jones, *Welsh Folklore* and *Folk-Custom* (Cambridge 1979 [1930]), 152, 158; Scotland: M. Macleod Banks, *Brit. Calend. Cust.* III, 1941, 16. Examples also found on the Continent.

8. See references given above. Also Halloween: Wirt Sikes, *British Goblins* (E. Ardsley, Yorks., 1973 [1880]), 214; Christmas: Mrs. Gutch, *County Folklore* II, *N. Riding* etc. (1901), 210–11.

9. See notes 7 and 8 above.

10. Eleven to one: Wright and Lones (1938) (note 7), 192; midnight: *Ibid.*, 190–91; between midnight and one: Rev. J. Gunn, 'Proverbs, Adages . . .' *Norf. Archaeol.* 2 (1849), 295.

11. Third vigil: Wright and Lones (note 7), 192. fasting: Macleod Banks (note 7), 16.

12. Forced to continue: R. Blakeborough, *Wit, Character, Folklore & Customs of the North Riding of Yorkshire* (E. Ardsley, Yorks. 1973 [1898]), 80–1 ('them 'at duz it yance awlus 'ev ti deea't; tha cann't ho'd thersens back, they're forced ti gan ivvery tahm St Mark's Eve cums roond.'); J. B. Partridge, 'Folklore from Yorkshire (North Riding)', *Folklore* 25 (1914), 376.

13. Church: Gutch (1912) (note 1), 65–66. Door: R. Whitlock, *The Folklore of Devon* (London, 1977), 158–59. Window: Wirt Sikes (note 8), 214. Porch: L. A. Law, 'Death and Burial Customs in Wiltshire', *Folklore* 11 (1900), 345.

14. Churchyard: Rev. G. S. Tyack, *Lore and Legend of the English Church* (London, 1899), 58–9. Lych gate: R. L. Tongue, *County Folklore VIII, Somerset Folklore* (1965), 145.

15. Lane: Gutch (1901) (note 8), 192. Crossroad: Blakeborough (note 12), 80. Window: Gutch (1901), 211.

16. Kendall: M. A. Denham, *The Denham Tracts* II (London, 1895 [1846–59]), 283–4. Winterton: Mrs M. G. W. Peacock, Folklore and Legends of Lincolnshire [ms] [pre–1929], 179 (available Folklore Soc. Library).

17. Similar 'dares' involved poking a stick in a tomb, or other ventures in churches or churchyards. Cf. K. M. Briggs, *A Dictionary of British Folk-Tales* B I (1971), 597–98.

18. T. Sternberg, *Dialect and Folk-Lore of Northamptonshire* (E. Ardsley, Yorks. 1971 [1851]), 188.

19. Aubrey (note 4), 207.

20. Wright and Lones (note 7), 191.

21. W. Hone, *Every Day Book* II (London 1878 [1827]), 275.

22. Gutch (1912) (note 1), 44.

23. Tongue (note 14), 170.

24. Peacock [ms] (note 16), 178–79.

25. G. Deacon, *John Clare and the Folk Tradition* (London, 1983), 283–84 (quoting an 1825 letter of the poet).

26. J. V. Powell, 'Folklore Notes from South-West Wiltshire', *Folklore* 12 (1901), 73.

27. Peacock [ms] (note 16), 179–80.

28. E. C. Gurdon, *County Folk-Lore Printed Extracts 2: Suffolk* (1893), 61.

29. Blakeborough (note 12), 80.

30. Tyack (note 14), 61.

31. E. Porter, *Folklore of East Anglia* (London, 1974), 61.

32. Tyack (note 14), 60.

33. See self: Law (note 13), 75; Incapable of glimpsing: J. Glyde Jr., *Folklore and Customs of Norfolk* (E. Ardsley, Yorks. 1973 [extracts from 1872], 24–25.

34. Denham (note 16), 283–84.

35. Deacon (note 25), 203–04

36. Glyde (note 33), 24–25.

37. Spirits: Gwynn Jones (note 7) 152; Ghostly voice: Wirt Sikes (note 8), 214. Devil: J. Simpson, *Folklore of the Welsh Border* (1976), 166.

38. R. F. B. Hodgkinson, 'Extracts from the Act Books of the Archdeacons of Nottingham', *Trans. Thoroton Soc.* 30 (1926), 52. K. Thomas, *Religion and the Decline of Magic* (London, 1971), 240–41, note 5, cites a 1584 example from the Consistory Court of Wells. It is not clear, however, that the church porch watch was the practice alluded to (see text at note 143 and note).

39. E. Peacock, *Glossary of Words used in the Wapentakes of Manley and Corringham* (London, 1877), 211–12.

40. Gutch (1912) (note 1), 44.

41. S. Baring-Gould, *Yorkshire Oddities* (London, 1890, rev. ed.), 22–27.

42. Hone (note 21), 275.

43–48. *Ibid.* 275–76.

49. J. Nicholson, *Folk Lore of E. Yorkshire* (E. Ardsley, Yorks. 1973 [1890]), 84.

50–52. *Ibid.*, 84–85, 92–93.

53. Gutch (1912) (note 1), 65–66.

54. gutch (1901) (note 8), 192.

55. Deacon (note 25), 284.

56. *Ibid.*, 288.

57. W. Henderson, *Notes on the Folk Lore of the Northern Counties* (E. Ardsley, Yorks. 1973 [1866]), 35.

58. W. H. Chaloner, ed., *Autobiography of Samuel Bamford* I, *Early Days* (London, 1967 [1849]), 160–62.

59. Heanley (note 6), 190–91.

60. W. Hone *Year Book* (London, 1878 [1832]), 408, 412.

61–65. *Ibid.*, 409–10.

66–67. *Ibid.*, 410–11.

68. H. Colley March, 'Dorset Folklore Collected in 1897', *Folklore* 10 (1899), 481 (recorded from Thomas Fox, aged 82).

69. Gunn (note 10), 292–93, 295 (apparently recorded from Mrs Lubbock, a washerwoman aged 80).

70. *Ibid.*, 295; Nicholson (note 49), 92–93.

71. Men: Henderson (note 49), 35. Women: *Ibid.*, 34–35. Object of dread: *Ibid.*, 35.

72. Somerset: Tongue (note 14), 170; Faroes: K. Williamson, *The Atlantic Islands* (1970 [1948]), 233.

73. Wright and Lones (1938) (note 7), 191; (1940), 19; Porter (note 31), 61; M. C. Balfour, *County Folklore* IV: *Northumberland* (1904), 55.

74. Mrs. Bray, *Traditions . . . of Devonshire* II (1838), 127–28.

75. Partridge (note 12), 376.

76. While this appears true of the majority of the cases, there is evidence in some of

a desire to see departed friends and loved ones: Powell (note 26), 72–73; Tongue (note 14), 171.

77. W. H. J. in *Folklore Journal* I (1883), 362.

78. Clerks and sextons: Glyde (note 33), 26; Wright and Lones (note 7), 190–91; Gutch and Peacock, *County Folklore* V: *Lincs.* (1908), 137; Physical position: Gunn (note 10), 295; Nicholson (note 49), 92–93.

79. Hone (note 60), 411.

80. Gutch and Peacock (note 78), 136.

81. Balfour (note 73), 55. Cf. J. Brand, *Observations on Popular Antiquities* I (ed. Ellis, London, 1890), 193.

82. C. Harvey, quoted W. E. A. Axon, 'The Church Porch', in W. Andrews, *Curious Church Gleanings* (London, 1896), 29.

83–87. *Ibid.*, 29ff.

88. H. Hubert and M. Mauss, *Sacrifice: its Nature and Function* (trans. W. D. Hall, London, 1964 [1898]); S. P. Menefee, Divination in the British Isles [ms] (1974, Oxford University), 221–22, 380–81.

89. Axon (note 82), 34.

90. F. J. Child, *English and Scottish Popular Ballads* I (New York n.d. [1882]), 220.

91. Tongue (note 14), 145.

92. S. P. Menefee, 'Circling as an Entrance to the Otherworld', *Folklore* 96 (1985), 10–11, 12.

93. Peacock [ms] (note 16), 179; S. P. Menefee (note 92), 9–11.

94. M. Puhvel, 'The Mystery of the Cross-Roads', *Folklore* 87 (1976), 167–77. Many love divinations could be practised in country lanes: Menefee [ms] (note 88), 86–87.

95. Menefee [ms] (note 88), 379–80; A. and B. Rees, *Celtic Heritage* (London, 1961), 83–94.

96. Tongue (note 14), 161; M. Trevelyan, *Folk-Lore and Folk-Stories of Wales* (E. Ardlsey, Yorks. 1973 [1909]), 254.

97. Menefee [ms] (note 88), 83, 379–80; Rees (note 95) 83–84, 89.

98. Peacock [ms] (note 16), 179; Menefee (1985) (note 92), 3ff. and [ms] (note 88), 91, 383.

99. This would strengthen the belief in the efficiency of the ceremony: Menefee [ms] (note 88), 420–22.

100. *Ibid.*, 409; E. Norbeck, *Religion in Primitive Society* (New York 1961), 94.

101. Menefee [ms] (note 88), 409–10.

102. *Ibid.*, 385–88.

103. Wright and Lones (note 7), 113; Macleod Banks (note 7), 130, 134–35, 150–51, 154; R. A. Firor, *Folkways in Thomas Hardy* (New York, 1968 [1931]), 46–47.

104. Deacon (note 25), 284.

105. A. D. H. Coxe, *Haunted Britain* (London, 1973), 115.

106. Aubrey (note 4), 143 (written c.1688–97).

107. See text at notes 79–80 and references given.

108. Menefee [ms] (note 88), 416–17. It stands to reason that those named by the watcher would include individuals expected to be approaching death; others named may have died through fear.

109. May 9, 1885, cited by P. H., 'Notes and Queries', *Folklore Journ.* 3 (1885), 279.

110. Whitlock (note 13), 159.

111. March (note 68), 481 (recorded from Thomas Fox, aged 82).

112. Peacock [ms] (note 16), 178.

113. Tyack (note 14), 61.

114. Gutch and Peacock (note 78), 137.

115. J. L. W. Page, *An Exploration of Exmoor* . . . (London, 1890), 34–35.

116. Gutch (1912) (note 1), 44.

117. *Ibid.*

118. Denham (note 16), 284. For similar beliefs connected with marriage divinations, S. P. Menefee, 'Master and Servant', *Folklore* 99 (1988), 88–97.

119. Rev. M. C. Morris, *Yorkshire Folk–Talk* . . . (London, 1911 [1892]), 225–26; *Athenian Oracle* 3, 515, quoted Brand (note 81) 3, 236.

120. See D 1825.6.1(a) (note 3).

121. Gutch and Peacock (note 78), 133. R. Chambers, *Book of Days* I (1883–86), 549, gives the name as Liveman Rapine.

122–123. *Ibid.*

124. Peacock [ms] (note 16), 179.

125. Hone (note 21) II, 275.

126. R. Hunt, *Popular Romances of the West of England* (London, 1923 [1881]), 385.

127. M. Baker, *Folklore and Customs of Rural England* (Newton Abbot, 1974), 148.

128. Bray (note 74), 127–28.

129. Tongue (note 14), 171.

130. Chaloner (note 58), 160–62.

131. Heanley (note 6), 190–91.

132. Scarborough: Henderson (note 57), 34–35; Westerdale: Morris (note 119), 225–26.

133. Nicholson (note 49), viii.

134. R. Bovet, *Pandaemonium, or the Devil's Cloyster* (1684), 216, quoted K. M. Briggs, *Pale Hecate's Team* (London, 1962), 200.

135. Brand (note 81) I, 331.

136. Peacock (note 39), 211.

137. *Ibid.*, 211–12.

138. J. Bowker, *Goblin Tales of Lincolnshire*, 198, quoted Briggs (note 17) B II, 505–06.

139. Tongue (note 14), 170.

140. *Ibid.*, 171.

141. Page (note 115), 312 (citing *Argosy*, Jan. 1870).

142. E. O'Donnell, *Haunted Churches* (London, 1939), 55–57.

143. Dom Aelred Watkin, *Dean Cosyn and Wells Cathedral Miscallanea* (Som. Rec. Soc. 56, 1941), 157. Thomas cites this in his discussion of the watch, but other divinatory rituals were of course engaged in on this date. Cf. Wright and Lones (note 7), 12ff.

144. Hodgkinson (note 38), 52.

145. Page (note 115), 34. An interesting contrast to this is the statement by Sikes concerning an aural form of the ritual in Wales: 'There are said to be still extant, outside some village churches, steps which were constructed in order to allow the superstitious peasantry to climb to the window to listen' (Sikes, (note 8), 214).

146. E. Porter (note 31), *Cambridgeshire Customs and Folklore* (London, 1969), 109–11.

147. S. Baring-Gould, *Further Reminiscences 1864–1894* (New York, 1925), 125 gives a further example.

148. Partridge (note 12), 376.

7

The Seer in Ancient Israel

J. R. Porter

The content of this essay is intended to conform fairly closely to its particular title and the general title of the volume. Hence it is concerned with the Israelite *seer* and hardly deals at all with the main prophetic figures of the Old Testament. As will be seen, the two cannot be wholly divorced from one another but it would be generally agreed that the great prophets represent a new stage in the development of Israel's religion and society; and anyway there are numerous studies of them to which a comparatively brief paper could hardly add anything of substance. Further, the seer will be considered only in the context of Biblical folklore, how seers and seer functions are depicted in popular stories about them. Of course these stories come to us now as part of the canon of Scripture, presented, as will be seen, in terms of the particular religious outlook of those who thought them worth preserving and writing down; it is, therefore, with the distinctively folkloristic elements still retained in them, often only incidentally, that we shall be solely occupied.

We may properly begin with a story, or at least part of it, the famous account of the anointing of Saul as king in chapters 9 and 10 of the first Book of Samuel, for it is here that we find a very interesting picture of the Israelite seer as he appeared to popular thought and expectation. The story in question is a quite distinct and self-contained unit and it is certainly basically a folk-tale.[1] It begins in the typical fashion of such tales 'now there was a man', the Hebrew equivalent of 'once upon a time'. Then the hero Saul is introduced in terms which bring out his qualities as they would appeal to the popular mind: 'a young man in his prime; there was no better man among the Israelites than he. He was a head taller than any of his fellows'.[2] Events are set in motion by the loss of some of the family's asses and Saul and a servant-companion set out to look for them: here is the theme of the quest or search. For three days, they traverse three lands, two of which at least defy any firm geographical indentification and may be intended to be deliberately mysterious,[3] but without success. Here, again, we seem to have that common theme of hero stories, the journey of the hero and the frustrations he meets in the course of it.⁴ Finally they reach a fourth mysterious land, the land of Zuph, and here Saul is minded to abandon the search, because his father will be beginning to forget about the asses and instead 'to worry about us'.

At this point, the servant comes up with a suggestion. In a neighbouring, though unnamed, town, he says, there is a man of God who is held in great honour 'because everything he says comes true', and the servant proposes that they go to him, since he may be able to tell them something useful to their errand. Saul agrees and, at this point, this man of God is described by the term 'seer', and later on he turns out to be the well-known figure of Samuel. But then we learn that the day before Saul came, Yahweh had told Samuel that a man from the territory of Benjamin would be sent to him whom he was to anoint king of Israel; and, as soon as Saul appears, Yahweh informs Samuel 'here is the man of whom I spoke to you'. So, finally, to the accompaniment of more deliberately mysterious episodes, Samuel anoints Saul and conveys to him Yahweh's assurance that he is to be Israel's king. Again, the climax represents a common theme in stories of this type, the hero achieving kingship, though it is noteworthy that, at the end of this particular narrative, Saul's true status remains secret until he has proved his worthiness for royal office by a heroic military deed which is recounted in the succeeding chapter.

Now this comparatively brief tale in fact reveals a good deal about the position and function of the seer in ancient Israel. Various discrepancies in it suggest that the identification of the seer in the story with Samuel is a later development, in accordance with the well-known tendency in the growth of folk-narrative for stories told originally about comparatively obscure figures to be transferred to more famous, and better historically attested, characters. Originally, the seer would have been anonymous and his town, which is never given a name in the narrative, is not to be viewed as Ramah, where the real Samuel had his home, but as some remote place in the mysterious land of Zuph. At the same time, the account is firmly rooted in the real life and concerns of old Israel. It shows us that the seer was an important and respected figure in society and that he took a leading role in the community's worship which had as much a social as a religious function.⁵

The seer's reputation rests on the fact that'everything he says comes true'. He is, so to speak, a sort of fortune-teller who can inform you of what you want to know. Indeed, as is commonly the case with seers, he knows what is concerning a person before he is even asked about it and, although the main thrust of our story is the revelation of Saul's royal destiny, it is made clear that the seer is equally authoritative in the lesser matter of lost property. When Saul and Samuel meet, the former asks,

'Would you tell me where the seer lives?' and the latter at once replies, 'I am the seer . . . Trouble yourself no more about the asses lost three days ago, for they have been found'.[6] Also, the seer is a professional who earns his living from his special skills: if you want to consult him, you have first to cross his palm with silver.[7]

Hence, it can be said, as a generalisation, that the seer is a person who claims to possess the faculty of knowing things that are concealed from ordinary people, and this includes the ability to predict the future. As we have seen, Samuel can foretell that Saul will become king but, also,when he takes his leave of him, he tells Saul that three events will occur whose significance is that they are signs which confirm his hidden destiny, and the account concludes with the words 'on that same day all these signs happened' — they clearly showed the seer's predictive gifts.[8]

We saw that the seer is also called 'man of God', where 'God' renders the Hebrew *'elōhîm*. Our English translations, with their capital G, refer the expression to the one true God. Certainly this is how *'elōhîm* would have been understood in later Israel and no doubt by the author of these chapters in their present form, since for him the source of Samuel's extraordinary knowledge is none other than Yahweh, God of Israel. But we may wonder whether this was the original connotation of the term 'man of God'. *'Elōhîm* in the Old Testament has a wide semantic field. As well as the one God, it can mean gods in the plural, it can mean the divine, or, perhaps, rather the supernatural in a general sense, it can be used as a superlative.[9]

Perhaps, then, the man of God is to be thought of as one who has the exceptional powers he enjoys because of his connection with, and knowledge of, the supernatural realm which lies behind and beyond the visible and tangible world. This frees him from the limitations of time and space, so that he sees events and circumstances which are hidden from ordinary human perception. All this would suggest that the Israelite seer was, at any rate to begin with, no different from similar figures known among the peoples surrounding Israel. Scholars have frequently called attention to the close similarities which can be demonstrated between the Israelite seer and what we can learn of seers among a wide variety of other peoples,[10] and this should not greatly surprise us.

We may now turn to the ways in which the seer actually operated, the ways in which he performed his functions. At the outset, it must be admitted that the evidence is comparatively scanty, but we can perhaps open up the question by considering another verse which now appears in the narrative of Saul's anointing: 'In days gone by in Israel, when a man wished to consult God, he would say "Let us go to the seer." For what is nowadays called a prophet used to be called a seer', I Samuel 9.9. This is clearly a sort of editorial note, reflecting a situation later than that of the original story.[11] Unfortunately, we cannot be certain either of its date or its background and much scholarly ink has been spilt in discussing its precise meaning.

Does it indicate merely a terminological change — 'new presbyter is but old priest writ large', as Milton put it — that is, there was just one type of holy man in Israel, who could be known by the general title 'man of God' but who was more specifically described as 'seer' in an earlier period but then as 'prophet' at a later one? Or were there, originally at least, two distinct types of 'men of God', with distinct, though no doubt overlapping, features, but that one, the prophet, replaced the other, the seer, in the development of Israel's life and religion? In favour of the first alternative, one can point to a number of passages where there seems to be no difference in meaning between the two terms, for example, 2 Samuel 24.11, 'the word of Yahweh came to the prophet Gad, David's seer' or the fact that, while Amos clearly belongs to the prophets, he is also addressed by the priest of Bethel as seer, Amos 7.12. However, the second alternative is perhaps more likely, provided that we recognise that while the role of the prophet became overwhelmingly predominant — there are only some twenty-eight instances of the word 'seer' in the Old Testament compared with hundreds of the term 'prophet' — yet the figure of the seer did not wholly disappear. Seers are still mentioned in the eighth-century prophets Amos, Micah and Isaiah, and, very interestingly, as late as the post-exilic writings of I and 2 Chronicles.[12] We can probably explain the decline of the seer from the fact that his methods of operation were closely identical with the divinatory practices of the Canaanites and other surrounding nations, as already observed, and, as is well known, such practices came to be strictly forbidden in the course of time in Israel.[13]

However, it is probably best to think of seer and prophet — and the same goes for other terms for various holy men in the Old Testament — not so much as different individuals but rather as denoting different functions, so that we might speak of the seer-function and the prophet-function. That is to say, there were different techniques or methods for acquiring and communicating the mysteries of the other world which were the common endowment of the holy man, the man of God.[14] One and the same person could well be expert in more than one of these techniques and employ different ones at different times as might be appropriate — so someone like Gad could easily be called both seer and prophet. We must always be careful with Israel, and indeed with the ancient Near East generally, not to think of the operations of holy persons overmuch in what might be called civil service terms, with clear lines of

demarcation and clearly defined functions. The supernatural knowledge
which the holy man possessed was essential for the *whole* of society's life
and so, as occasion demanded, he could answer the needs and demands
of society in what are, at least for us, quite different capacities — so, for
example, the *kāhin* of the pre-Islamic beduin Arabs was seer, prophet,
priest, judge and military leader all in the same person,[15] and the same
can be said of the Old Testament also.[16] As we have seen, Samuel is a seer,
dealing with matters of ordinary peasant concern, but he is also concerned
with high affairs of state, 'the matter of the kingdom', I Samuel 10.16.
As we also saw, he is a priest and elsewhere in the material about him he
is called a prophet and shown as exhibiting the distinctive phenomenon
of prophecy, what is usually called ecstasy.[17] Also, however, he is very
clearly a judge, hearing legal cases,[18] and he appears as the head of the
army in a holy war.[19] Of course, one can speak, as scholars have done,
of a growth of a Samuel legend cycle and ask whether all these traits in
fact belonged to the one historical personage. What is important from
the standpoint of this essay is that the Biblical tradition could view, quite
naturally and without incongruity, all these characteristics as combined
in a single individual.

If we are correct in what we have said about seer-function and
prophet-function and the religio-historical relationship between them,
it follows that in the Old Testament the dividing line between seer and
prophet cannot be drawn too sharply and that 'what is nowadays called
a prophet' took over many of the methods and functions of the seer,
thus allowing us, when we seek to investigate the Israelite seer, to use
certain evidence from the activities of those whom the Bible describes as
prophets. But in order to do this, we have first to discuss a little more
fully just what were the *distinctive* modes of operation of the seer, just
what is the seer-function. Once more, the question is not altogether an
easy one.

The term 'seer' in our translations of the Old Testament renders
two different Hebrew words, *rō'êh* and *ḥōzêh*, and these are the active
participles of the verbs *rā'âh* and *ḥāzâh*, both of which mean 'to see'.
When we survey the comparatively infrequent use of *rō'êh* and *ḥōzêh* in
the Old Testament, it is difficult to see any difference between them,
and most scholars think there is none. It has been suggested that the
distinction is merely a dialectical one, but there is no evidence for this
and, when we meet different terms in the Bible which now seem to mean
much the same, it is always worth asking whether this was originally the
case or whether they did not once indicate distinct entities. We may
perhaps find a clue from the two verbs from which *rō'êh* and *ḥōzêh*
respectively derive. *Rā'âh* is the ordinary word for the ordinary act

of seeing and it therefore occurs frequently. *Ḥāzâh* is much rarer and it is virtually confined to poetry in the Old Testament. This may well be significant, for there is the closest connection between poetry and prophecy: it is in the exalted and mysterious language of poetry that the prophet speaks.[20] So the two verbs may, at least originally, have meant two different methods of perception of that supernatural world to which the seer is privy, and *rō'êh* and *ḥōzêh* would denote two different specialisms, a *rō'êh*-function and a *ḥōzêh*-function, so to speak. *Rā'âh* is used for ordinary and prophetic seeing, while *ḥāzâh* rather has the sense of a mysterious perception belonging to the realm of the numinous.

Before going further, it must be made clear that this distinction, supposing it to be there at all, cannot be pressed too far, and there are certainly a few instances in the Bible where *ḥāzâh* seems to be used of quite ordinary seeing, for example Proverbs 22.9, 'Do you see (*ḥāzâh*) a man skilful in his work? He will stand before kings'. Nor, to revert to a point made earlier, is it meant to imply that one and the same seer could not exercise both the *rō'êh*-function and the *ḥōzêh*-function, though different individuals might be specialists in one or the other. All that is being suggested is that there are two modes of seeing which the seer could use.

The difference between them may be illustrated from the story in Numbers 24 of the famous Balaam who is there depicted, though a foreigner, with many of the characteristics of the Israelite seer.[21] In the chapter, we first read that 'he saw Israel encamped tribe by tribe', v.1. This is perfectly straightforward seeing and the verb *rā'âh* is used; but, of course, it is mentioned as one of the seer's special capacities, for, as the sequel shows, the sight of Israel's tents acts as an omen which triggers off a prediction of the future prosperity of the nation and this reflects a common prophetic technique in the Old Testament. But then, significantly, we come to a poetic passage:

> the oracle of the man whose eye is opened,
> the oracle of him who hears the words of God,
> who sees the vision of the Almighty,
> falling down but having his eyes uncovered, vv. 3–4.

Surely here we are confronted with something rather different and the verb for seeing is *ḥāzâh*. Here we may properly speak of the numinous, the direct vision from God experienced in the physical phenomena of the trance.

And what may confirm the suggested distinction between *rā'âh* and *ḥāzâh* in the case of the seer is the fact that the latter verb is much less closely linked with real bodily seeing than is the former. To give just one example, the prophecies of Amos, Micah and Habbakuk are all introduced by the same formula, 'the words of So and So which he saw' (*hāzâh*). Now obviously this is not literal seeing — one does not see words — and the real sense is well brought out by the New English Bible's translation of Amos 1.1, 'the words of Amos which he received in visions': we may compare the similar introduction to the book of Isaiah, 'the vision' (from the root *hāzâh*) of Isaiah which he saw' (*hāzâh*).

Now visions or dreams — it is not easy to draw a sharp line between them[22] — as the means by which the seer or prophet gains his knowledge of that reality hidden from other beings are so well attested in all cultures, and certainly in that of Israel, that it is hardly necessary to dwell on them at any length. But it is perhaps worth spending a little time on discussing some of the other characteristic means by which the seer's special perceptive faculties are exercised, as we find them in Old Testament stories. The indications of these are often small incidental elements in such tales, so that they have frequently been overlooked and their particular significance not realised. One modern scholar has listed the chief methods used by Israelite seers as 'dreams, extraordinary perspicacity, clairvoyance, communications from ghosts and spirits, and finally, external signs and omens'.[23] Leaving aside dreams, and also communications from ghosts and spirits,[24] let us take first 'extraordinary perspicacity'. The Biblical writers who have shaped and transmitted the narratives we are considering were convinced believers in Yahweh and so they naturally regard the seer's gift as depending on a special endowment from him: we might be more inclined to speak of an innate quality. But, in any case, we are to think of a permanent and regular faculty possessed by the individual in question. Here, however, we must remember what was said above about the danger of confining the possession of special spiritual endowments to particular categories of persons. So we should not think — and it is indeed a rather obvious point — that extraordinary perspicacity was the prerogative only of certain professional groups, such as the seer in I Samuel 9. It could characterise a wide variety of individuals and in them too it was attributed to a special divine endowment.

To illustrate the point, we may take an episode from the reign of David, recounted in 2 Samuel 14. The situation is that David has banished his son Absalom for the murder of his brother but Joab, David's right-hand man, wants him restored to favour. So Joab sends to the town of Tekoa for a 'wise woman' from there and instructs her: 'Pretend to be a mourner . . . then go to the king and repeat what I tell you', and then 'he told her exactly what to say'.

Three things may be observed here. First, we are clearly dealing with a professional, a female seer of whom we meet several examples in the Old Testament:[25] she is described as wise because she had knowledge beyond the ordinary, as was characteristic of the seer, and her services were available to clients. Secondly, we see here a very down-to-earth, not to say sceptical, attitude to the seer's pretensions, which we find not infrequently in other societies than Israel: if the seer's counsel is, as we have seen, valued in high affairs of state, then he or she is always liable to be manipulated by astute politicians, as again we find happening elsewhere. Thirdly, Tekoa may have been one of the places where seers congregated and where their professional skills were learned and transmitted. The prophet Amos, who is also called a seer, came from there and there is a possibility that he was a member of a class of professional diviners. In 2 Samuel 20, Joab is besieging the town of Abel-beth-maacah, and another wise woman of the place seeks to dissuade him from destroying it by quoting a well-known proverb: 'In the old days, there was a saying "Go to Abel for the answer" and that settled the matter'. This suggests that Abel too was a place with a long succession of seers who could provide answers to the problems of those who resorted there to consult them.

To return to the tale of the wise woman of Tekoa, she presents herself to David and tells her story of how one of her own two sons has killed the other, so that,by the custom of blood-revenge, he is in danger of being put to death by her relatives. When David promises that his life will be spared, she goes on to suggest that he should act in the same way towards his own son Absalom. At this point, David says to her: 'Tell me no lies . . . is the hand of Joab behind you in all this?' Her reply is significant: 'Yes, your servant Joab did prompt me . . . your majesty is as wise as the angel of God and knows all that goes on in the land'. Now, one can rightly say that here we have an instance of the shrewdness which made David so capable a ruler and even that, since Joab had probably been at him already, it would not have been particularly hard to guess who had put the woman up to it. But for her David's perspicacity is extraordinary. Just as with the seer, it is a result of a divine endowment: David is as wise as 'the angel of God', a term which in the Old Testament denotes the channel through which the deity reveals his purposes and intentions in the human world.[26] Just like the seer, he has exceptional knowledge: nothing of whatever happens in his entire kingdom is hidden from him.

What all this suggests is that in the Bible it is not always easy to distinguish native shrewdness and quickness of mind from genuine examples of clairvoyance or second sight, any more than it is in the case of the modern medium. Nevertheless, to come to the next item in our list of the seer's characteristics, there are a number of instances in the Old Testament where genuine clairvoyance does appear to be attributed to him. Before considering a few of them, two more general observations may be in order.

First, basing ourselves on the etymology of the terms for 'seer', we have so far concentrated on the role of seeing in the activity of that personage. But one must be careful not to lay too great stress on this, on second *sight*, on clair*voyance*. Recent studies of Hebrew psychology have shown that its conception of the human personality was a very fluid one, marked by what has been called a diffusion of consciousness, so that the functions of one organ could easily be transferred to another.[27] So, as has already been noted, one can 'see' words and, although Samuel is a seer, yet we are told that his awareness of Saul's impending visit was because 'Yahweh had uncovered his ear'. It might be better, then, to view the seer not so much as one who sees, though of course he is that, but rather as one who perceives, by whatever means he is thought to do this.

Secondly, we now have to make use of evidence drawn not just from the comparatively rare mentions of actual seers in the Bible but much more from what we are told of prophets. However, as we have noted more than once, a sharp line cannot be drawn between seer and prophet and the latter often retained much of the methods and characteristics of the former. This is especially true of the pre-eighth century prophets, like Elijah and Elisha, who represent a kind of transitional stage between the older seer and the fully developed phenomenon of Israelite prophecy. It is to these we now turn.

In the popular stories which make up the folkloristic cycles about Elijah and Elisha, we have several examples of clairvoyance or second sight. Elisha was able to frustrate the Aramaean plan of attack because he knew, he had heard, the words the king of Aram said in his bedchamber.[28] On another occasion, he saw, heard and recognised men who were approaching before their arrival.[29] With this may be compared the very interesting story of the visit of the wife of king Jeroboam I to the prophet Ahijah.[30] She had come to consult him about her son's illness and Ahijah is clearly a professional seer in a modest way of business, for she takes a comparatively small gift to pay for his services, ten loaves, some raisins and a flask of syrup. However, her husband was on bad terms with Ahijah, who thus might refuse his help, so she disguises herself,[31] but as soon as he heard her footsteps at the door, Ahijah called out 'Come in, wife of Jeroboam'. What is interesting is that we are told that Ahijah was blind. The blind seer is a figure met with in other societies and this trait is surely present to emphasise that the seer's perception does not depend on ordinary human sight but is internal and supernatural. In the Biblical story, Ahijah, like Samuel, knows who his visitor really is because Yahweh has already told him but, in view of other instances of second sight, such as those already mentioned, we can fairly attribute this again to the theological outlook of the final narrator.

Two other instances of clairvoyance are recounted of Elisha. On one occasion, he confronted his servant Gehazi, who had secretly accepted a present from the healed Naaman, when Elisha had refused it, and then lied about it, with the words: 'Went not my heart with you when a man turned back from his chariot to meet you?'[32] In the Old Testament, the heart often represents the total human person, so Elisha had actually been with Gehazi and seen what happened.[33] Noteworthy, however, is the somewhat vague statement — Elisha only saw 'a man' turning from his chariot[34] — and this corresponds well to the indistinctness and studied mysteriousness of such cases of clairvoyance. On another occasion, the king of Aram falls sick and sends Hazael, his chief minister, to Elisha to enquire whether he will recover,[35] this time with a more splendid gift, forty camel loads of all kinds of wares of Damascus. In response to the enquiry, Elisha replies: 'Go and tell him that he will recover, but Yahweh has revealed to me that in fact he will die'. This is a good example of the ambiguous oracle which the seer may give, attested elsewhere in the Old Testament, and, of course, well-known in other areas:[36] for the king did not die from his illness but was murdered by Hazael. But then we read that 'Elisha fixed his gaze and stared at Hazael', language which indicates strong emotion,[37] and burst into tears. When asked why, he answers that it was because he knew the terrible damage Hazael would do to Israel when he succeeded as king. What is pictured here is the way in which an ordinary visual experience, the sight of Hazael, triggers off a trance in which the harm that Hazael will do is vividly present to the seer's inward eye.

This last instance leads on to a consideration of another item in our list of the methods used by the seer, 'external signs and omens'. Perhaps, for the purposes of this essay, enough has already been said about omens and how they operate, but external signs deserve a little further attention. On the one hand, natural phenomena, as we might call them, can have revelatory significance for the seer: there is plenty of evidence for this in the Bible but here attention will be confined to a single case which has not, it would seem, been considered in this light hitherto. Before Elijah on Mount Horeb,[39] there passed wind, earthquake and fire, but, though it might have been expected, 'Yahweh was not in these', they were not on this occasion the medium of revelation for the seer. Then, however, Elijah hears 'a low murmuring sound', an obscure expression and perhaps a deliberately mysterious one. It has plausibly been suggested that it refers to the rustle of the desert breeze, but it is at the same time the whisper from the other world — there is no mention of Yahweh being in it — which the seer's ear alone can catch, as we know from what is said of the practices of diviners mentioned elsewhere in the Old Testament.[40] That this is so is shown by Elijah's reaction. He went out and stood at the entrance of the cave where he had taken shelter, no doubt to hear better, and 'muffled his face in his cloak'. We can understand why he did this when we recall that the pre-Islamic Arab *kāhin*, to whom reference has earlier been made, covered himself with a veil when he was engaged in seeing. The desert breeze was indeed the external sign of the presence of the supernatural and its message. Of interest also is the final part of the narrative of the event in Elijah's life immediately preceding the one just discussed.[41] The country had suffered a drought for several years but now Elijah says to king Ahab: 'I hear the sound of coming rain'; he has a vivid precognition of it. But the mere prediction is not enough. Elijah orders his servant to go and look out for the coming rain and he does this seven times, a common folklore pattern, but meanwhile Elijah ascends a mountain and there 'crouches on the ground with his face between his knees'. It has been suggested that this was an act of imitative magic, where the prophet simulates a rain cloud, but it is perhaps more likely intended to induce concentration: in any case the posture can be paralleled from the practice of seers and clairvoyants from other areas.[42]

On the other hand, the seer may have made use of external signs in the sense that he employed material objects in divination. There is not a great deal of evidence about this in the Old Testament, though again it would correspond with what we know of the ways of seers elsewhere. However, this kind of divination was certainly characteristic of the Israelite priesthood and we have seen that, in early Israel at least, no sharp division can be made between seer and priest either. In this connection, attention has often been drawn to the Mesopotamian figure known as the *bārū*. The verb *bārū* means 'to see' or 'to behold': the *bārū* is one who has the power of seeing in a special way and thus corresponds very nearly to the Hebrew seer. The means used by the *bārū* included the receiving and interpretation of dreams, but they were primarily of a technical nature, such as the observation of oil and water in a cup,[43] the way objects fall when thrown, the entrails of sacrificial animals, celestial phenomena and the movements of animals and birds. Further, the *bārū* formed a particular class among the priesthood in Mesopotamia: he was intimately connected with the temple cult and hence scholars commonly speak of the *bārū*-priest.

What we seem to find in Israel is an increasing division and specialisation, between different groups, of functions which at an earlier date were found together in the person of a single undifferentiated holy man, 'the man of God'. So no doubt the fully developed Hebrew priesthood was clearly distinguished from the seers and the Hebrew sacrificial cultus in the Biblical descriptions of it has certainly lost all divinatory significance. But there are indications that such was not always the case,[44] and it has been suggested that at one time the Israelite priest may have been very like the Babylonian *bārū*.[45] And — leaving aside the clear evidence in the case of Samuel — there is one passage where a priest may be called a seer. When Absalom's revolt compelled David to flee Jerusalem, he was joined at the outskirts of the city by Zadok, the chief priest, and a group of Levites carrying the sacred ark. David orders them to return with the Ark to Jerusalem but then says to Zadok, according to most English translations, 'Are you not a seer?'[46] Unfortunately, both the text and its meaning are uncertain. The word used is *rō'êh*, which, as we noted, is a verbal participle and thus it may not be used here in a technical sense. So the New English Bible has: 'Can you make good use of your eyes?', that is, 'I want you to act as a spy in the enemy occupied city', a rendering which gives excellent sense, because a few verses later David instructs another prospective spy that he is to report to Zadok and his fellow priest Abiathar, who will then arrange to transmit his information to David. Nevertheless, we cannot wholly rule out the possibility that Zadok is here called a seer in the technical sense and thus approximates to the *bārū*. He was the guardian of the Ark and the Ark seems to have been used for oracular enquiries.[47] Seer and spy need not be mutually exclusive; we have already observed that the seer's position could be exploited for political purposes.

It is only possible to deal very cursorily with a few other aspects of the seer as he appears in Israel's popular traditions. There are many famous stories of him as a remarkable healer, like the Japanese seer described elsewhere in this volume. Sometimes the seer or prophet appears as little more than a skilled herbalist, as when Elisha throws in some meal to neutralise a pot of poisonous herbs[48] or Isaiah orders a fig-plaster to be applied to king Hezekiah's boil.[49] But one of these healing stories, the narrative of Elisha and the Shunamite woman,[50] merits discussion in a little more detail, because it incidentally throws a good deal of light on the nature and functions of the seer-prophet.

The tale begins with a wealthy lady providing Elisha with a room in which to stay on his regular visits. This she did because he was 'a holy man of God', which shows his great significance in society. To have such an important person under her roof would bring prestige and good fortune, as is confirmed later on in the story when Elisha asks the woman how he can repay her: 'Shall I speak for you to the king or to the commander-in-chief?' But all she wants is a son, which Elisha promises, and the child is duly born. This suggests the seer as the giver of fertility, a theme we find in several other stories about both Elijah and Elisha.[51] But eventually the child dies and the woman asks her husband to saddle an ass so that she can go to Elisha for help. Her husband replies: 'Why go to him today? It is neither new moon or sabbath' — the seer is a professional practitioner who had regular consulting hours on the holidays, the holy days, when people did not have to go to work and could visit him. However, the woman persists and when she interviews the prophet, Elisha orders his servant: 'Take my staff in your hand, go with her and lay my staff on the face of the child. If you meet anyone on the way, do not give him a greeting and if anyone gives you a greeting do not return it'. Here we find the seer's magical staff — the rods of Moses and Aaron also come to mind — and it is infused with a mysterious power which Arabs would call bᵉrākhāh, blessing.[52] When you greet a person, you convey some of your bᵉrākhāh to him but on this occasion every drop of it, so to speak, is needed for the mighty task of bringing the dead to life.

But the servant's mission failed and Elisha, the real source of bᵉrākhāh, had to come himself to save the boy. The description of what he then did is so interesting that it deserves detailed quotation. Elisha entered the bedroom, shut the door on the family and prayed to Yahweh: the seer works in secret, partly in order not to betray his methods but also so that his concentration may not be disturbed. 'Then, getting on to the bed, he lay on the child and put his mouth upon his mouth and his eyes upon his eyes and his hands upon his hands; and as he crouched over the child, the flesh of the child grew warm.' The seer's own vital force, a quasi-physical thing, is conveyed to the dead body through all its vital organs. And hence the seer needs, so to speak, to re-charge his batteries, for we next read that 'Elisha got up and walked once up and down the room; then, getting on to the bed again, he crouched over the child and breathed into him seven times; and the boy opened his eyes'. The seer may sometimes act spontaneously but often he has to work hard, he may not succeed at once and he perseveres with established techniques: these are all features which characterise the operations of seers in many societies.

By way of conclusion, we may mention just two other particular characteristics of the seer. Elijah apparently had the capacity to move with mysterious rapidity from place to place. So the royal servant Obadiah complains that he will never be able to be sure where Elijah is, for 'as soon as I have left you, the spirit of Yahweh will carry you off I know not where',[53] or when his fellow prophets cannot find him they fear that 'perhaps the spirit of Yahweh has lifted him up and cast him on some mountain or into some valley'.[54] The expression 'lifted him up' suggests that Elijah was thought to be able to fly through the air, and we read of this happening several times to the prophet Ezekiel,[55] whose career seems to mark a recrudescence of some of the experiences of earlier seers.[56] It was the same supernatural power, described this time as the *hand* of Yahweh, which impelled Elijah, after his rain-making on Mount Carmel, to run all the way to Jezreel, outpacing Ahab's chariot, when the king was driving at top speed to get home before the thunderstorm made the road impassable.[57]

Secondly, Dr MacInnes refers to the fact that Scottish seers could either inherit their gift or acquire it. There is no real evidence for the former in the Old Testament: the expression 'the sons of the prophets' has sometimes been interpreted as implying a hereditary succession but it probably means no more than belonging to the category of prophets. But individuals were certainly admitted into the prophetic office by their predecessors. Elisha was chosen as a prophet, when, out of the blue, Elijah threw his cloak over him,[58] and, when Elijah was assumed into heaven, Elisha inherited this cloak, together with a double portion of Elijah's 'spirit', his mysterious, quasi-physical power.[59] This latter gift was promised to him only if he saw Elijah being taken up into heaven: perhaps we should understand that this was really a visionary experience which would prove that Elisha was a true seer. The role of the cloak in all this is significant. Clearly it had the same sort of power as we noted in the case of Elisha's staff, but also, together with the tonsure[60] and some sort of incision on the forehead,[61] it was what marked off the seer. It was a sheepskin or goatskin such as is worn by nomads and it was already an archaic costume in the settled Israel of Elijah's day. Holy persons throughout the world often don special clothes, which were once only the ordinary dress of the community, and they are cherished and handed on to their successors, as Elijah's mantle was to Elisha.

Much more could be discussed but it may be hoped that our survey has given some impression of the part played by the seer in early Israelite society. We have largely concentrated on the 'professionals', since they are easily distinguishable, but perhaps enough has been said to indicate that, beyond them, the seer *function* was much more widely known and recognised in that society. The value of the Old Testament popular tales at which we have looked is precisely the way in which they reveal how those with the special endowment of 'seeing', in its various modes, actually operated in the circumstances of ordinary life; and in this respect those stories are virtually unique in the ancient Near Eastern world.

NOTES

1. The best description of the story's genre remains that of H. Gressmann, *Die älteste Geschichtsschreibung und Prophetie Israels*, 2nd edit., 1921, 34.

2. I Samuel 9.2.

3. Cf. M. Bič, 'Saul sucht die Eselinnen, I Sam ix', *Vetus Testamentum*, vol. VII, 1957, 95; H.I. Stoebe, 'Noch einmal die Eselinnen von Kîš (I Sam. ix)', *ibid.*, vol. VII, 1957, 363.

4. Cf. J. R. Porter, 'Heroes in the Old Testament', ed. H. R. E. Davidson, *The Hero in Tradition and Folklore*, 1984, 104.

5. I Samuel 9.11–13; 22–24. We should probably think of the occasion as a clan feast, cf. W. R. Smith, *The Religion of the Semites*, 3rd edit., 1927, 239.

6. I Samuel 9.18–20.

7. I Samuel 9.6–8.

8. I Samuel 10.2–9.

9. Cf. D. Winton Thomas, 'A Consideration of some Unusual Ways of Expressing the Superlative in Hebrew', *Vetus Testamentum*, vol. III, 1953, 209 ff.

10. Cf. J. Lindblom, *Prophecy in Ancient Israel*, 1962, 83ff.

11. It appears to be a marginal gloss, which has crept into the text at the wrong place, since it annotates the word 'seer' which occurs for the first time only in verse 11, cf. Peter R. Ackroyd, *The First Book of Samuel*, 1971, 76.

12. Amos 7.12, Micah 3.7, Isaiah 29.10; 30.10, I Chronicles 9.22; 9.29; 25.5; 29.29, 2 Chronicles 9.29; 12.15; 16.7; 16.10; 19.2; 29.25; 29.30; 33.18; 33.19; 35.15.

13. Cf. the discussion by J. R. Porter, 'Ancient Israel', in edd. Michael Loewe and Carmen Blacker, *Divination and Oracles*, 1981, 192–5. When the priest of Bethel addressed Amos as 'seer', Amos 7.12, he was not intending to be polite to him and was probably aiming to link Amos with those who had come to be regarded as illegitimate diviners.

14. Cf. J. R. Porter, *op.cit.*, 199.

15. Cf. the fundamental essay by Johs. Pedersen, 'The Role played by Inspired Persons among the Israelites and the Arabs', in ed. H. H. Rowley, *Studies in Old Testament Prophecy*, 1950, 127–142.

16. Cf., for example, A. Malamat's description of the Israelite 'judge', in ed. B. Mazar, *The World History of the Jewish People*: vol. III, *Judges*, 1971, 130.

17. Cf. I Samuel 3.20; 19.20.

18. Cf. I Samuel 7.15–17.

19. Cf. I Samuel 7.5 ff.

20. Cf. particularly H. Gunkel, 'The Prophets as Writers and Poets', in ed. D. L. Petersen, *Prophecy in Israel*, 1987, 31.

21. For Balaam, cf. J. R. Porter, (note 13), 199 f.

22. Except perhaps the distinction drawn by Johs. Pedersen, *Israel: Its Life and Culture, I–II*, 1946, 140, 'there is only the difference between them that the vision is received when awake', though one might prefer to say that the dream is received only when asleep.

23. J. Lindblom, *Prophecy in Ancient Israel*, 1962, 94.

24. The present writer has discussed this topic in his essay 'Ghosts in the Old Testament and the Ancient Near East', in edd. H. R. E. Davidson and W. M. Russell, *The Folklore of Ghosts*, 1981, 232–7.

25. The closest parallel is the wise woman of Abel-beth-maacah, referred to below, but one can also cite the prophetesses Deborah, Judges 4.4, Huldah, 2 Kings 22.14, and Noadiah, Nehemiah 6.14.

26. Cf. W. Eichrodt, *Theology of the Old Testament*, vol. II, 1967, 23–9.

27. On the whole subject, cf. especially A. R. Johnson, *The Vitality of the Individual in the Thought of Ancient Israel*, 1949.

28. 2 Kings 6.12.

29. 2 Kings 6.32–33.

30. I Kings 14.1–18.

31. Probably the smallness of the payment was part of the queen's attempt to present herself as an ordinary woman: in her real capacity she would have been expected to be more lavish – contrast the typical Oriental generosity to a prophet of a great man like Naaman, 2 Kings 5.22–3.

32. 2 Kings 5.26.

33. Compare the New English Bible's translation: 'Was I not with you in spirit when the man turned back?'

34. The current English translations do not render the Hebrew literally.

35. 2 Kings 8.7–15.

36. Cf., for example, Gressmann's explanation (note 1), 280, of the ambiguity of the prophecy of I Kings 22.6, which he compares with the famous response of the Delphic Oracle to Croesus.

37. The New English Bible brings it out well: 'Elisha stood there with set face like a man stunned'.

38. For a fuller discussion, cf. J. R. Porter (note 13), 195–7.

39. I Kings 19.9–14.

40. Cf. G. Hölscher, *Die Profeten*, 1914, 84ff.

41. I Kings 18.41–46.

42. Cf. John Gray, *I & II Kings*, 1970, 403f.

43. We may compare the wise man Joseph who was a dream expert but also had a cup to divine with, Genesis 44.5.

44. Cf. J. R. Porter (note 13), 207f.

45. In the description of the priestly family of Levi at Deuteronomy 33.8, it is noteworthy that the first thing mentioned is the possession of the Urim and Thummim, that is, the objects used for divination.

46. 2 Samuel 15.27.

47. Cf. I Samuel 14.18.

48. 2 Kings 4.41.

49. Isaiah 38.21.

50. 2 Kings 4.8–37.

51. Cf. I Kings 17.13–15; 2 Kings 4.1–7, 42–44.

52. For this, cf. Johs. Pedersen (note 22), 182–212.

53. I Kings 18.12.

54. 2 Kings 2.16.

55. Cf. Ezekiel 2.14; 11.1,24 and note especially 8.3.

56. Cf. also the legend of the prophetic Habakkuk in the apocryphal book Bel and the Dragon, 33–36.

57. I Kings 18.44–46.

58. I Kings 19.19–21.

59. 2 Kings 2.8–15.

60. Implied by 2 Kings 2.23.

61. Implied by I Kings 20.41.

8

The Seer as a Healer in Japan

Carmen Blacker

The word for clairvoyant vision in Japan is *gantsū* or *reigan*. The people possessing this gift are able to see the spiritual beings from another world which intermingle with our own. These beings can affect our lives, both for good and for evil, in crucially important ways, yet to ordinary eyes they remain invisible. The seer through his gift of second sight can communicate with these beings, thus forming a bridge of vital importance between our own world and the invisible world.

In this paper I propose to examine the following points. How does the seer in Japan acquire his gift of clairvoyant sight? What kind of training is necessary in order to develop this special power? And how are these powers deployed for the benefit of the community, particularly when that community is part of a modern industrialised society?

An ancient premiss of Japanese culture is that most of the ills of this world have their cause in invisible spiritual beings which impinge forcefully on the human community. The chief cause of ill therefore lies in another dimension, out of reach and out of sight of ordinary men and women. These beings comprise, first, ancestral ghosts whose descendants have not been diligent enough in performing the necessary requiem obsequies, and who are hence neglected, starved and angry. A second source of danger lies in certain animals — foxes, badgers, snakes and occasionally dogs — who are capable of entering into the human body in invisible form and causing a variety of sicknesses and sufferings. A third possible danger lies with the divinities known as *kami*, who again, if neglected or flouted, can cause a variety of miseries — sickness, bankruptcy in business, failure in university entrance examinations, quarrels, sterility and singleness.

It is therefore vitally important to have someone in your midst who is capable of seeing the beings of this spiritual world, and diagnosing the cause of the ill. Without a specialist seer, you are terribly vulnerable to attack. You are incapable of telling who is causing the misfortune, and for what reason they are attacking their victim. You are incapable hence of taking any steps to remedy the situation.

116

Let us look at a few examples of the manner in which the seer in Japan practises his or her art.

Presented with a patient complaining of some pain or sickness that does not respond to ordinary medical treatment, the seer must first diagnose whether or not it is in fact caused by spiritual agencies, and is not simply an obstinate case of lumbago or neglected cough. He must then discover what spirit is causing the trouble, and what its reasons are for attacking the patient. Having ascertained these crucial facts, he can proceed to persuade the being to cease its attacks, so that the patient can recover.

Mrs Nakano, a professional healer and ascetic from Shikoku, told me in 1963 that for her cures she relied chiefly on her faculty of *gantsū* or second sight. No sooner was her patient seated before her than the image of a fox, or a resentful ancestor, or an enraged *kami*, would appear before her seeing eyes. Or, should the case not be one of spiritually caused sickness, she would see, equally clearly, the image of an inflamed appendix or an overtaxed liver. She would then enter into a dialogue with the spirit, ascertaining first why it should attack the patient, and then, by a combination of cajolery, bargaining and scolding, persuading it to leave its victim.

Another seer whom I met in 1963 was Mr Mizoguchi, who lived at the foot of Mt Miwa near Nara. He too could cure sickness through his faculty of *gantsū*. A man had recently come to him who had suffered from epilepsy for twenty-one years. Mr Mizoguchi recited the Heart Sutra, and at once the images of two unhappy ancestors rose before his eyes. One had been drowned, the other had died in a mountain fire. Neither had received the correct requiem rites, and hence neither had been able to achieve rest. They were therefore persecuting their descendant with epilepsy in order to draw attention to their plight. Mr Mizoguchi performed the correct obsequies, and the man had no more epileptic fits.

Mr Mizoguchi's powers included that of seeing whether a tree or a stone were holy or not. He could see at once if a *kami* had taken up residence in a certain rock or pine tree, and indeed, when I climbed Mt Miwa with him during the summer of 1963, he was kind enough to point out to me which trees and rocks were thus inhabited, and which therefore demanded special reverence and respect. This faculty was an important one if sacrilege, with all its unfortunate consequences, was to be prevented.

Another celebrated seer and healer in the Nara district was Mrs Hiroshima Ryūun, who accomplished many dramatic cures during and immediately after the war. In her manuscript diary, lent to me by her daughter in 1972, a number of disturbing cases were recorded. One example will have to suffice. Mrs Hiroshima was summoned to a house where the baby was suffering from an obstinate and painful swelling on the shoulder. Mrs Hiroshima recited the Heart Sutra, and at once three spirits appeared before her seeing eye.

'Who are you?' she asked them.

'We used to live in this house,' they replied. 'But we all died young and poor. We had no descendants to perform the proper rites for us, and hence we are starved and suffering, unable to achieve buddhahood. We made the baby sick in order to draw attention to our plight. Say the right sutras for us, and we will let the baby get well. Our graves are south of this house.'

The baby's father then remembered that an uncle of his had been buried near the house, with two wives who had died one after the other childless. No one had performed the right obsequies for them, so that it was natural that they should adopt such ferocious means to call for help.[1]

We may note here that the gift of second sight is often accompanied by another faculty, *mimitsū* or clairaudient hearing. The seer is enabled not only to see the invisible beings, but to converse with them, listen to their stories and suggest remedies.

The question now presents itself: how are these useful gifts acquired? Is a person born with them, or are they acquired as a result of spiritual disciplines?

The answer seems to be a combination of the two. You have to possess a certain natural predisposition towards such powers. But at the same time training of a strictly traditional kind is essential.

Persons gifted with second sight, and making their living as healers, usually exhibit a life history along the following lines. Their childhood and youth are dogged by poverty, misery and sickness. These miseries rise to a culminating crisis, in which a spiritual being takes them in complete charge. This being, which always names itself at its initial dramatic appearance in vision, dream or possession, announces that the person has been specially chosen to be its instrument, and that henceforth his slightest move will be ruled by this Guardian spirit.

There follows a period of severe austerities, *gyō*, commanded and supervised by the Guardian. A diet restricted to the products of trees, *mokujiki*, was not uncommon. No meat, no salt, no cereals, only bark, nuts, pine needles and roots, was the rule. Cold water ablutions, particularly during the cold winter months, were likewise prescribed. The candidate is ordered to stand under a waterfall for a prescribed period every day, or to tip large buckets of cold water over head and body. At the same time he or she must recite, with all the force at his or her command, a holy text. The text most valued for this purpose in medieval times was the Lotus Sutra. In later centuries mantras, *dharani*, the Heart Sutra, or the *nembutsu* or invocation to Amida, were extensively used.

After several months or even years of such austerities, the seer's powers will have developed and consolidated, and the Guardian allows him to settle down in one place to practise as a seer, healer and exorcist. The period of *gyō*, it should be stressed, is essential to the full development of the seer's powers. No one will trust a seer who has not accomplished a full programme of *gyō*. Conversely the man or woman who has undergone a specially severe programme of *gyō* will carry greater prestige as a seer and healer.

We now pass to the question how are such powers still deployed in the Japan of today? How are such ancient gifts useful in a country with a booming economy, ever expanding industry, and a developing medical practice? The answer appears to be that they are useful as never before. The traditional belief in the proper treatment of the dead, and in their power to affect our lives, far from dying out, has asserted itself in a number of new ways.

An example is the strange new cult of the ghosts or embryos, killed in abortions or miscarriages.

In Japan since 1949 abortion has been extremely easy. Before 1949 the practice was forbidden under the Eugenic Protection Law, but since that date there have been neither legal prohibitions nor religious sanctions to hamper it. Nor, until some ten years ago, was it attended by any sense of guilt. Several of my friends who married during the 1950s had two or three abortions, because family planning was not readily available and the pill not yet invented. The total figure for abortions given by the Ministry of Health for 1960 was approximately a million, though by 1979 the availability of contraception had brought the figure down to half a million. Indeed, abortion during the 1950s was generally regarded as more morally desirable than a sprawling unplanned family.[2]

But when I visited Kyoto in 1981 after an absence of three years, I noticed a strange proliferation of Bodhisattvas heralded as saviours of *mizugo* or embryos. A new statue of *Mizugo Kannon* or a *Mizugo Jizō* seemed to have arisen in many temples where none had been before. A little investigation revealed that during the preceding eight or nine years an entirely new cult had arisen and spread with remarkable rapidity. Its principles were as follows.

According to the ancient tradition already discussed, many of the sufferings and calamities of this world are believed to have their causes in another invisible world. They are the work of discontented ghosts of *kami*.

But now a new kind of ghost had appeared on the scene, the ghosts of all the *mizugo* or embryos who had been killed in abortions during

E

the thirty years since 1949. These now ran into millions, and were very virulent because for all those years they had been not only completely ignored, but also deliberately forgotten and suppressed. They had been given no name, no requiem of any kind, and had been wandering in a dreary limbo of neglect and starvation for sometimes decades. The time had come for them to draw attention to their plight.

Further investigation revealed that a flourishing headquarters for the new cult existed in a temple not far from Kyoto called Emman-in. I visited it at an early opportunity, avowedly on behalf of a friend, who, distressed about an abortion she had undergone twenty years previously, was anxious to avail herself of any comfort that might be provided.

I found that an established procedure existed. You paid a sum of money to the temple, which in return gave the embryo ghost a name, and put it under the protection of the resident Bodhisattva Kannon. A small tablet was made, black lacquer with the ghost's new name in gold letters, and every Tuesday afternoon a ritual called *nyūkonshiki*, or 'rite for implanting the soul', was performed which safely housed the ghost in this new refuge. The fee was five thousand yen for a year of such protection, and fifty thousand for the service in perpetuity.

The afternoon I visited Emman-in happened to be a Tuesday, so that I was lucky enough to witness the commitment of some six hundred black and gold tablets. The temple had, I was told, an average of six hundred new souls to look after every week.

The tablets were then enshrined in an extensive area behind the altar. I was amazed to see room after room opening out, the walls lined with black and gold tablets. There were also several couples, a little furtive, who had come either for consultation or to make offerings to their own ghost tablets.

Afterwards I spoke with the officiating priest, and here it is that seership comes in.

He told me that often a couple would come to him, requesting the temple's help for one embryo-ghost or perhaps two. Soon he felt a tap on his shoulder, and turned round to see two more small embryo-ghosts who said, 'Don't forget us!' He would then ask the couple if they were sure that it was only one embryo that they wished to commit to the care of the temple.

Shamefacedly the wife would then confess that there were two more, which she had never mentioned to her husband. Thanks therefore to the priest's gift of second sight, the family was henceforth properly looked after, and need expect no further molestation from embryo-ghosts.

Such temples are now, eight years later, extremely numerous. Their number certainly runs into thousands, if not to tens of thousands.

Emman-in alone dealt not only with six hundred new tablets every week, but also with fifty thousand visits of enquiry every year, not to speak of providing a twenty-four hour dialling system with recorded advice.

How this new cult was first started is by no means clear. But no sooner had it made its appearance than it became obvious that a great deal of money was to be made — by any temple providing a convincing saviour bodhisattva, or by any 'specialist' offering advice through books and private consultations. Such 'specialists' advertise prominently in women's magazines and on television. Their business flourishes because the entire structure and pattern of the cult they profess is so ancient and deeply embedded in the culture.

An example of the current literature is *Mizugo no Himitsu*. (Secrets of Embryo Ghosts), published in 1980 by Nakaoka Toshiya. Mr Nakaoka claims to be a specialist in the cure of sicknesses caused by embryo-ghosts, and he is a seer in so far as he *sees* the spirits with whom he is dealing.[3]

Here are two of the cases he describes.

A girl came to him suffering from awful stomach cramps and giddiness. She confessed that she had had no fewer than five abortions, one every year since the age of fifteen, and was yet again pregnant. Mr Nakaoka explained that on no account must she have another abortion, and that she must take immediate steps to have the necessary rites performed which would bring the ghosts of the other five to comfort and salvation. She must do this whether her husband agreed or not, for it was her only chance of cure. The stomach pains and giddiness were the direct result of the vengeance of the five ghosts.

The girl took his advice, and two months later was back, happy and smiling, all trace of sickness gone.

Another young wife, after a second abortion, began to suffer from terrible period pains in which her legs went numb and her back hurt appallingly. What was more, frightful quarrels had begun to break out between her and her husband, who also had been sacked from his job.

Mr Nakaoka could at once *see* that the trouble was caused by the two ghosts, and prescribed obsequies which very soon cured the wife's pains, caused the quarrels to cease, and reinstated the husband in his job.

A good many books have appeared of this kind, which can be easily bought on station bookstalls. They point out forcefully and repetitively that the whole range of miseries to which the human condition is subject can be plausibly attributed to the work of embryo-ghosts seeking revenge and restitution. The mother may expect gynaecological troubles, stomach pains and an overpowering urge to suicide.[4] The father may be warned of traffic accidents, cancer, vicious drinking habits and an addiction to gambling. The other children in the family tend to lose energy, to do badly at school and to develop odd allergies. There is also a general tendency to family suicide.

All these risks can be easily obviated by following the advice of the specialist or the temple.

The *mizugo* cult is only one among many new religions which ascribe the origin of calamity and suffering to discontented ghosts, which offer diagnosis through a seer for the cause of the malady, and a ready cure through a ritual to placate the unhappy beings. These new cults are flourishing, with a constant influx of new members and patients, and constant employment for anyone gifted with the powers of *gantsū*.

In the Japan of today therefore we see a remarkable example of the seer's powers not only surviving in a modern industrialised society, but even given new value and respect. Out must go the view, therefore, which used to hold that 'magic' was incompatible with science, that progress in science would automatically destroy the magical view of the world; that magic occupied a lower rung of a ladder which must necessarily be left behind when a society advanced into scientific rationality. In Japan the two views of the world coexist without difficulty. Indeed, the gifts of the seer are now more openly acknowledged and accepted than they were a dozen years ago. Twelve years ago, before Japan had proved herself to be not only rich and successful, but to have outstripped the West in technology and industrial power, the methods of the seer in combating evil in our lives were much less overtly accepted. Religion and magic, for anyone with pretensions to modernity, were dubbed pre-modern, anti-rational, against progress, and above all likely to provoke unflattering comparisons with the West. To be modern meant to be rational, and to be rational meant to reject the entire world of spirits, and the powers of those who claimed to see its inhabitants.

Since Japan has by general consent outstripped the West in technology, and since there is no longer any need for her to compete on this front, she can now safely drop the persona of rationality in spheres where it was never truly believed. The old explanations for sickness, misfortune and disaster can safely reassert themselves, and the seer's function can once more be openly acknowledged. The gift of *gantsū* in Japan is thus a boon. The man or woman so gifted is a bridge between our own world and the invisible one which impinges so closely on ours. The gift is thus regarded with none of the suspicion, the numinous horror, the sense of illicit prying into places properly hidden from man's sight, that prevails in many Christian countries. Nor is there any fear that the gift proceeds from an evil source. On the contrary, the man or woman possessing supernatural sight is welcomed in the community as one who commands a faculty invaluable for the common good.

NOTES

1. I have written at greater length on this subject in my *Catalpa Bow* (London, 1975), chapters 2, 12 and 15.

2. See the useful article by Mary Picone, 'The Mizugo Rei Cult, Irrational Revival or New Teleology', 1984, unpublished, p. 12. It is commonly alleged that since 1949 there have been 50,000,000 abortions carried out in Japan. See also i) Anne Page Brooks, "*Mizuko Kuyō* and Japanese Buddhism", *Jap. Jour. Religious Stud.*, 8, 3–4, Sept. 1981. ii) Hoshino Eiki and Takeda Dōshō, "Indebtedness and Comfort: the Undercurrents of *Mizuko Kuyō* in Contemporary Japan," *Jap. Jour. Religious Stud.*, 14, 4, Dec. 1987. iii) Bardwell Smith, "Buddhism and Abortion in Contemporary Japan: *Mizuko Kuyō* and the Confrontation with Death", *Jap. Jour. Religious Stud.*, 15, 1, March 1988.

3. Nakamura Toshiya, *Mizugorei no Himitsu*, Tokyo, 9th printing 1981. In an appendix the writer gives a list of the principal temples throughout Japan offering services to exorcise *mizugo*, with addresses and telephone numbers. The number has certainly doubled since the book was published, and old temples such as the Hasedera at Kamakura now add substantially to their income proclaiming this extra virtue for their bodhisattva.

4. The urge to commit suicide is said to be particularly strong on the anniversary of the abortion. Picone (note 2), p. 26.

9

The Chinese Tradition of Prophecy

Michael Loewe

China's literature, historical records and religious archives may well be regarded as extensive or even voluminous; but if a general statement may be risked, there would appear to be a notable absence of attention to named figures of certain types which feature prominently in the cultural heritage of the West. It may well be asked whether there are Chinese counterparts to prophets who, like Isaiah or Amos, convey the revealed word of God; or to leaders such as Moses who, by possession of the gift, may determine the fate of communities; or to recognised seers such as Teiresias, Merlin or Rasputin whose powers command the respect and call for obedience by masters of the nations. Similarly while there is a profusion of sites which were regarded as holy and made over for worship of the gods, there would appear to be few or no sites famous for the frequency of the prophetic utterances which they evoke, of the same class as Delphi, Dodona or Epidaurus.

This apparent absence in Chinese mythology, folklore and history is more than compensated for by the profuse information concerning the means of prophecy, the instruments upon which prophecy depends and the titles which distinguished those whose specialist skills or ritual functions came to form an integral part of mantic processes. Whereas in the western tradition renowned individuals whose gift became manifest at crucial moments of history are named, in the Chinese tradition we meet the gift as part of the stock-in-trade of a whole variety of professionals, be they Masters of the Way, intermediaries or specialists in the use of a particular set of instruments.

Written evidence of prophecy and its techniques is seen in a variety of forms. There are archival records, i.e. documentation produced during an act of divination and not intended for further circulation; there are historical statements, i.e. narrative accounts of incidents in which oracles were consulted, duly set out as an historical record; there are lists of the officials of a kingdom or an empire who were duly charged with responsibility for conducting mantic ceremonies; but how far such lists should be judged to be real rather than ideal may well be a matter of doubt.

While the Standard Histories certainly include biographical accounts of some intermediaries who were engaged in a variety of activities, these individuals are treated with far less attention than that accorded to officials of state. Chinese literature also includes some of the criticism that was voiced in respect of certain practices and the naive faith that they inspired, and there are lists of technical manuals which concern their operation. Prophecies, when disclosed, usually take the form of pithy sentences, which may not now be entirely comprehensible; declamatory texts such as those of *Daniel* are hard to find.

Specialists in the occult arts included several types who might claim the gift of prophecy. There were the *daoshi*, or Masters of the Way, whose self-training was directed to achieve comprehension of and conformity with the mysteries of the universe. While the results of their powers of prediction were not usually disclosed in public, they are perhaps the most genuine type of seer in the tradition; they are also those of whom we know least. There were also specialists who were engaged in interpreting the manifest signs of oracles or in inducing signs to appear by various processes of divination; and there were those who were skilled in the use of man-made instruments, manuals or almanacs.

Seers should be distinguished from other masters of the occult, such as shamans, prayer-makers or exorcists who also feature in the Chinese tradition. They were concerned with pronouncing whether a proposed action would meet with good or bad fortune; to do so they sought guidance by way of three types of phenomenon which were not necessarily kept distinct in the Chinese mind. i.e. oracles, divination and omens. They would consult oracles by searching for features of the natural way of the world and by interpreting the signs inherent therein; or they would practise divination by deliberately inducing certain patterns to take shape in material form, as a result of what appeared to be random activities; or they could recognise the internal message carried by strange phenomena of the heavens or the earth that were of such conspicuous or immediate consequence that they could not be ignored. The lessons to be learned from such omens may have been signs of good or of evil; probably they would be of general significance to the whole community.

Consultation of oracles and the practice of divination were known at all levels of Chinese society, whether official or popular. A search for guidance by these means merited the trust of emperors and officials; of generals leading their forces in battle; of farmers seeking how best to use their land or where best to situate their homesteads or their ancestors' graves. Outrageous acts of nature, or omens, necessarily became the concern of royal or imperial authorities, requiring placatory action, and thus requiring mention in dynastic histories as portents. The earliest written records that China boasts, of *c*.1700 BC, consist of accounts of acts of divination, stating the occasion for such acts, the purpose of the enquiry and its results; considerably more detailed information exists for historical times. In general the following remarks are based on evidence dated not later than 200 AD, with the proviso that many elements of early practice have survived much later and may even be witnessed today.

In the earliest known method of divination to be practised in China, turtle shells or animals' bones were exposed to a fierce heat. Already cut, trimmed or otherwise worked, the material had been considerably weakened, with the result that the heat induced cracks to appear. Depending on the size, shape, position or number of the cracks, so would the seer pronounce the answers received from shell or bone in response to specific questions that had been put. The seer was thus interpreting signs whose appearance had been deliberately stimulated by human means, in a manner that could not be subject to control.

Acts of divination were performed on behalf of the kings of Shang, and once completed a record of the incident was engraved on the material that had been used.[1] From such inscriptions we learn that the questions which were put could be factual, such as whether the prospects for the harvest were good or bad; or they would concern the outcome of a project, e.g. of hunting or a campaign. A high proportion of the questions concerned the appropriate timing for an act of worship or sacrifice, or for other activities. Sometimes a matter of choice was put forward, e.g. that of an heir, wife or concubine. What is unknown is the precise way in which a pattern of cracks related to the seer's interpretation; but we are safe in assuming that, at least in the early stages of the practice, the role of the seer was esoteric and not subject to dispute.

No material evidence survives from early times for the second of the major methods of divination, which was practised from perhaps 800 BC and is widely used today. From a group of fifty stalks of a rare and highly venerated plant, often identified with the yarrow, the operator would divide off smaller groups, until he was finally left with a remainder of one, two, three or no stalks. Dependent on that remainder he would then draw out, according to a recognised usage, a pattern formed of six horizontal lines; acknowledged prescriptions provided that a line would be of one of two types, either whole, or split into two halves. The total number of hexagrams that could be constructed in this way is thus sixty-four. However, a further complexity enters in as each one of the lines was regarded as being either static or actively mobile; such a quality was inherent in the cast of the stalks and the resultant number of those remaining after the throw.

Once the specialist operator had cast his stalks and formed the hexagram the seer took his part in the proceedings by pronouncing an interpretation or prognostication of what this arbitrary or random process and its emergent lines foretold. Such pronouncements would, it was hoped, have a direct bearing on the question that had been specifically put for guidance.

Divination with the use of yarrow stalks has had highly significant intellectual and literary implications in the development of Chinese thought and science. These appeared, in the first instance, in the compilation known as the *Yijing*, or *Book of Changes*, which includes some material that may date from perhaps 600 BC, together with a number of accretions and commentaries of considerably later times.[2] Such developments, which continue with much vigour until the twentieth century, are more the concern of philosophy than the seer and his methods, and attention should now be focused on other considerations.

As with the use of shells and bones, so with the stalks of the yarrow plant divination depended on signs that were made manifest as linear patterns. In both methods the diviner's role was similar; he drew on esoteric sources of wisdom and his utterances were beyond the reach of reason or argument. Like the cracks formed on the shells, the hexagrams could give guidance that would apply to particular questions at issue, and there has probably always been a considerable stress on choosing the most suitable or auspicious moment for embarking on a project. In addition the material substances that were employed as the medium of the seer were believed to be repositories of deep wisdom acquired throughout the very long life of the turtle or the yarrow and manifested in the latter's exuberant growth.

From divination, the deliberate fabrication of signs by man, let us turn to oracles, the consultation of signs already existing in nature if man but takes the trouble to look for them. There need be no great difficulty in so doing, as these signs form part of the normal and regular phenomena of the world, as may be seen in the case of the clouds and the winds.

It has long been the habit of some Chinese to discern patterns, such as the forms of animals or other objects, in the shape of the clouds, and to infer prognostications for the future from such pictures. As contrasted with divination by shells or stalks, we possess late evidence only for consultation of the clouds, beginning from shortly after 200 BC. By that time the practice had already been subject to a degree of formalisation, to which we shall revert later, but it can only be assumed that the practice had arisen from earlier and less standardised forms; and there may be reason to believe that certain types of specialist were thought to possess the gift of interpretation.

The objects that the clouds were thought to be depicting included animals, human beings, mythical creatures such as dragons, man-made objects such as carriages, wheels or articles of clothing. From evidence that is comparatively late we learn of interpretations of these signs, in a rather stylised manner, with reference to the fortunes of war, or the dangers of violence.

As with the clouds, so with the oracles of the winds the evidence is late and the part played by the seer is more a matter of assumption than direct knowledge. Depending on the time when the winds arose, their quarter of origin, their direction and their force, so could a seer prognosticate certain activities, such as the outbreak of fire or of armed rebellion in a particular area. In addition, if interpreted correctly winds could be a guide to the prospects for the harvest, climatic changes or seasonal disasters of flood or drought. If it is duly observed at crucial points in the calendar, such as the New Year's Day, the behaviour of the winds may indicate the fortune that is likely for the whole of the incoming year. An interesting statement of Yi Feng, a man of learning and a statesman of the first century BC, sheds some light on the way in which these oracles were regarded. He wrote that 'winds are the proclamations of heaven', and his statement is not entirely unique. We are thus not concerned with prophets to whom there was vouchsafed a personal knowledge of the message of God; we are concerned with phenomena or features that carry such revelation within them, ready for the seer to interpret.[3]

Omens were extraordinary, abnormal and often catastrophic events whose incidence was far too obvious to evade attention, let alone to require a positive attempt to find them. They included eclipses of the sun and the moon, landslides, the growth or decay of crops out of season or reversals of the normal climatic sequence. Alternatively an omen could be an event which inspired hope rather than fear, such as the fall of honeydew or the appearance of a rare and noble animal. But in both cases, whether they were omens of disaster or of felicity, they were matters which could not be left solely to the private consideration and pronouncement of a visionary seer. Unavoidably they were brought into the forum of public discussion. Being events that could concern the welfare or survival of man, they must perforce be reported to senior officials and finally to the emperor himself. Set in the glare of publicity, interpretation could often be directed so as to accord with contemporary prejudice, to reflect political animosity or to follow discussion on intellectual lines; but omens were not the preserve of the dogmatic utterance of the seer who possessed the gift.

Nonetheless events which may be regarded as omens are not entirely irrelevant to Chinese mantic practices, if only because certain incidents were open to treatment either as a source of oracle or as an omen. Comets form a good example of such events. Recently found evidence shows how, by 200 BC, they were being treated in two ways. As parts of the regular order of nature they were classified and provided with written prognostications thought to be appropriate, in just the same way as the various shapes seen in the clouds. As with the clouds, so with comets it is possible and even likely that such treatment followed an earlier stage when it had been the part of the seer to pronounce upon the meaning of these normal phenomena, and classification may well have been a secondary and subsequent development. Alternatively there are records which show that comets could equally well be treated as extraordinary events which were duly reported to the throne as harbingers of an emergency and which gave rise to solemn discussion of their significance.

It has been observed that divination with the use of stalks gave rise to intellectual and literary results; that consultation of the oracles of the clouds and the winds became subject to stylised interpretation; and that the appearance of omens became a matter for official recognition, intellectual debate and political action. From such developments it may be seen how the treatment of mantic activity proceeds in China. It starts as the concern of visionaries whom a king trusts to pronounce a message from occult sources open only to those with the gift; it becomes subject to official and intellectual influences which reduce age-old spontaneous procedures to occasions which are marked with formality; and in this process the qualities of integrity and validity may disappear. Such developments could hardly be avoided in view of the characteristics that were emerging in Chinese thought as the centuries passed and human institutions were becoming more and more sophisticated and complex. Divination, oracles and omens could not be separated from the whole concept of human destiny and man's place in the universe.

By the second century BC, if not before, there had grown up the view that all observed phenomena, whether in the heavens, on earth or in the sphere of human activity, formed parts of a single, unitary universe. Different situations arose in the cosmos in direct correspondence with the stages of an ever-repeating cycle. That cycle could be defined or imagined in several ways; in general it could be seen in terms of birth, death and rebirth; in more particular terms it was seen as a series of sixty-four moments or situations, symbolised by the sixty-four hexagrams that had started life as patterns formed in the process of augury. Divination with the use of stalks thus came to be directed to identifying a particular stage reached in the cycle and determining whether it would be appropriate for a proposed action. Time was viewed as being circular rather than linear; much of the purpose of putting questions to shells or yarrow stalks, or of reading the signs inherent in the clouds and the winds, was to determine the right moment in time and its cycle.

Other ideas that were being formulated in the last few centuries before the present era were likewise affecting mantic processes. These included the concept of Yin and Yang as the pulsating forces that maintain life and the operation of the universe, working through the agency of the Five Phases (*wu xing*) of being. There was also the concept of *qi*, a life-giving, life-inspiring but invisible energy,whose influences may be seen to underlie all nature and to inform all manner of being.[4] In addition the overriding Chinese love of classification and hierarchies was finding expression in and application to all matters and activities of the heavens, earth and man. As a result, activities that had been basic to treatment as signs from the occult became evidence to be reviewed in the light of philosophical or scientific theory. Intellect and a search for order was taking the place of reliance on a seer's gift.

A more mechanistic approach towards mantic procedure emerges in a number of ways. Almanacs were compiled in tabular form, showing successive days in the calendar; for each one a note specified those projects that would be successful and those which should be avoided. According to the circumstances of birth, an individual could consult the appropriate almanac for guidance, e.g. when to embark on marriage, when to move house or when to travel. Another method depended on the use of instruments, comprising circular or square discs which were used in combination; around the perimeter of the boards there were inscribed several concentric series of symbols, sometimes in the form of animals, but usually as written characters. Such instruments could be set in accordance with the time and place of the enquiry, and a pointer would designate the appropriate member of the series on the perimeter which indicated the requisite advice. By this means it was hoped to ensure that an individual's choice of action was consonant with the major rhythms and movements of the heavens and the earth.

As is known from recent archaeological finds, such instruments were in use from the second century BC at least. This was still some thousand years before the evolution of the magnetic needle, which was perhaps first mounted on instruments of this type from the eleventh century. A new departure in usage accompanied that advance. Hitherto instruments had been used to determine the appropriate time for taking an action; with the obvious lead given by the faculty of the magnetic needle the new instruments came to be used to determine a choice of place rather than time, e.g. the choice of a suitable site for burial, rather than a suitable day. In this way the instruments came to play a decisive part in Chinese geomancy (*fengshui*), which endeavoured to ascertain whether a defined site on earth would be subject to good or evil influences. Possibly, in the remote past, it had been the part of the seer to recognise the characteristics of the land for such purposes.[5]

Further signs of the move away from the inspired utterances of the seer to consultation by standardised means may be seen in the detailed codifications that were drawn up for various methods. These documents specified the correct procedures to be followed; e.g. they prescribed ways of preparing the turtle's plastron, subjecting it to fire, distinguishing the emerging lines and interpreting their meanings. It cannot be told for certain why such manuals were drawn up in the first instance. Possibly they were intended for apprentices; alternatively they may have acted as a *vade-mecum* for a charlatan whose pretensions to the gift could be detected only too easily, should he have no ready store of recondite guidance on which he could draw.

Finally the establishment of a whole complement of specialist officials, each with his defined responsibilities for carrying out part of the ceremonies of divination, tells its own story. These men were appointed to serve their emperor by ensuring that careful attention was paid to detail and to the requisite procedures. They figured in the lists of officials alongside specialists in other matters that demanded technical proficiency, such as prayer, sacrifice, music and medical practice.

These developments are a far cry from the response of the gifted seer who knew instinctively the meaning that lay behind the cracks on the turtle's shell, or the cast of the yarrow stalks. We may well believe that those seers possessed some unconscious understanding of these linear patterns that is denied to other mortals; they may have maintained an esoteric link or relationship with the holy medium of shell or stalk. By virtue of their age such objects could almost be regarded as permanent, and thus as repositories of wisdom, in a world peopled by transient creatures. There may well be little stress in the Chinese tradition on the person of the seer, while greater importance is paid to the process of prophecy, its mechanisms and its regulations. It is in any event significant that some of the practices which began shortly after 2000 BC survived for many centuries, adulterated as they were by intellectual and official pressures, but despite a full measure of criticism from Chinese sceptics.

NOTES

1. This archive first came to light at the beginning of the twentieth century; for a study of the inscriptions, see David N. Keightley, *Sources of Shang History: The Oracle-Bone Inscriptions of Bronze Age China* (University of California Press, 1978).
2. For translations of this enigmatic text, see *The I Ching or Book of Changes: the*

Richard Wilhelm Translation rendered into English by Cary F. Baynes (London, 1951, in two volumes; third edition 1968, in one volume); and John Blofeld, *The Book of Change* (London, 1965). In consulting these translations it is essential to discriminate between the different portions of the text. The earliest parts are written in language which was partly obsolete and whose meaning had been forgotten by the start of the Christian era. The later parts of the text, which date from within a century or so of that time, set out to explain the meaning of the earliest parts in philosophical terms that had been formulated at a much later period than that of the original parts.

3. Biographies of specialists in the interpretation of these signs and in other occult arts were included in the Standard Histories for the first four centuries of the common era; for translations, see Ngo van Xuyet, *Divination, Magie et Politique dans la Chine Ancienne* (Paris, 1976); and Kenneth J. De Woskin, *Doctors, Diviners and Magicians of Ancient China: Biographies of Fang-shih* (New York: Columbia University Press, 1983).

4. For the implications of the Five Phases, or Elements, and concepts such as *qi*, see Joseph Needham, *Science and Civilisation in China*, volume 2 (Cambridge, 1956), 232f; and Ho Peng Yoke, Li, Qi *and* Shu: *An Introduction to Science and Civilization in China* (Hong Kong University Press, 1985).

5. For *fengshui*, see Stephan D. R. Feuchtwang, *An Anthropological Analysis of Chinese Geomancy* (Vientiane: Editions Vithagna, 1974).

10

The Role of the Seer within the
Punjabi Asian Minority of Britain

Venetia Newall

The *Oxford Dictionary* defines a seer as: 'one to whom divine revelations are made in visions', 'a magician', 'one who has the power of second sight', 'a crystal-gazer', 'an inspector'.[1] All these meanings are relevant to the functions of the seer within the Punjabi Asian minority community of Britain.

Estimated at approximately 1½ million, the Asian minority in Britain is the largest non-white community and represents 2% of the total population. It is mainly composed of individuals who are from, or whose ancestors were from, the Indian sub-continent, who are scattered over the country in small numbers. The most substantial concentrations occur in such urban areas as: the East End of London, Walthamstow and Southall (both part of the London sprawl), Birmingham, Bradford, Leicester and Glasgow. Punjabis are conspicuous among these groups. They originate from a wide range of professions, occupations, economic backgrounds, colour groupings, and religious affiliations. They have brought with them, and have transmitted to the second generation, belief in evil spirits, the evil eye, magic, and witchcraft, which is regarded as both the means of prevention, and the cure for: physical illness, economic and social failure, difficulties in family relationships, and the destruction of enemies, and their power to do harm.

The prevention and curative aspects consist of: burning herbs to provide auspicious fumes of inhalation; drinking specially prepared liquids; chanting; praying; burning pieces of wood or cloth; blood-letting; emetics; purgatives; and massage. Techniques used to drive out evil spirits include: name-changing; charms and holy phrases inscribed on paper, soaked in liquid, which is then consumed; charms spoken over nails, which are placed in specially designated parts of the house; prayer; and formulas administered by professionals, devised to counteract the effect of evil influences. Traditional methods of prevention, protection, and healing are not always convenient or even possible in Britain. New forms have therefore been devised by professional practitioners, who are consulted for reasons often very different from those meaningful on the Indian sub-continent.

The data consists of case-studies. Through the network of various communities an attempt was made to use the technique of participatory observation for this investigation. The Asian press also indicates the existence of magical belief and practice in the form of publicity, news items, and readers' letters. Findings reveal that belief in witchcraft and magic, sometimes stronger than faith in scientific medicines, cuts across all religious groups and has no relevance to levels of education, experience, economic status, colour, or gender.

It is interesting that virtually all the fortune-tellers and faith-healers who advertise in *West Indian World*, the leading West Indian newspaper, are either Indian or Pakistani. The first example of a practitioner, whom I shall refer to as A, who lives in West London, came originally from Lahore, Pakistan. His father-in-law was a well-known practitioner of magic, and his wife also enjoys the reputation of being a magician. By trade he is a carpenter and used to work in a factory, but now he is self-employed. This occupies him during normal working hours, but, at weekends and in the evenings, he sees clients and helps them to overcome ill-health, difficulties in personal relationships, and a variety of other problems. His four-bedroomed house, decorated with ornate inscriptions from the Koran, is well-appointed, but A is planning to move, because it is insufficient to accommodate his rapidly expanding clientèle; many have to wait outside in the street until it is their turn for a consultation.

A sits in the front reception room, his wife in the back, and both receive clients. As a rule the women consult his wife, but some will go to A. In this specific instance 80% of the clientèle are women. It is important to make an appointment, otherwise there will be a long delay, since sixty to eighty people call in need of help in the course of each week.

A receives one client at a time. But, if a married couple, two friends, or relatives, come together, they may be seen simultaneously. Time spent on each varies from five minutes to half an hour. A sits on the floor, his clients on the sofa. He greets them in the Muslim style of the Indian sub-continent, asking their name and approximate date of birth. He then casts a horoscope, using a reference book, and asks about the client's specific complaints and problems. Typically these fall into the following categories: illness (pains, aches, depression); nightmares; fears; the indifference of children and their problems regarding dating outside the community; the coldness of husbands; job loss and unemployment; the common disappointments of everyday life.

Observations and diagnoses are usually: (1) someone has performed witchcraft (2) the client has inadvertently stepped on a malevolent charm

(3) the client has been captured by a roving evil spirit (4) vague and very generalised reference is made to the past history of the client, emphasising any outstanding successes or failures.

The client's problems are usually attributed specifically to one of the following: (1) charms have been soaked in water which the client drank (2) charms were burnt in the client's home (3) charms were deposited in the client's kitchen, or lavatory, or tied to the door (4) harmful spells have been chanted (5) human ash has been deposited in the client's house (6) the client inadvertently consumed human ashes (7) the blood of a bird was sprinkled on the client's body or in the house (8) charmed nails were deposited in the client's house.

Remedies follow set patterns. A recites something unintelligible over a bottle of water, which is then given to the client with instructions to sprinkle it in the house during a given period of time. The client must wear a charm in a metal case, or burn it, or soak it in water and drink the liquid. A recites another charm, as he waves a small stick over the client, especially over parts of the body described as painful or afflicted in some way. He then blows over the client, who is sometimes asked to recite portions of the Koran.

A is popular and respected. Though he is a Muslim, many of his clients are Sikhs and Hindus. He does not claim any hereditary or family rights, nor does he assume superiority over other people. He is not involved in any political activity and makes no demands for money. Clients may pay nothing, or as much as £100.

B, a second, contrasting, type of practitioner, claims to originate from the Syed dynasty, which migrated from Arab lands and settled in the Indian sub-continent many centuries ago. He comes from the Punjab, Pakistan, is Imam of the local mosque in an outlying area of London, and wears traditional dress with a long beard, which is symbolic of a religious figure of standing within the Muslim community. Many Pakistani immigrants in Britain come from his part of Pakistan, and he was sent over to serve as Imam for the mosque, and for the local community.

Since his area is far from the Central London Mosque, all Muslims who wish to pray attend his mosque, especially on Fridays, the Muslim holy day. Because sermons at the Central London Mosque are in either Arabic or English, languages not easily understood by the majority of the older immigrants, B enjoys two advantages: he is readily accessible, and he speaks the same language as his congregation. The majority of immigrants in his part of London are from the rural Punjab, and their exposure to Western education is limited.

B, who is known as both Mavlana and Shah Sahib, titles for Muslim holy men, speaks with great confidence and authority, and explains his command over a variety of Islamic subjects by reference to his direct descent from the family of the Prophet Mohammed. His Friday afternoon congregations run into thousands. He only arrived in England five years ago, but it is estimated that he has already acquired property worth £75,000, in addition to sending several hundred pounds a month home to his family back in Pakistan; his declared regular income from the mosque is very small.

He is well-known among his followers as someone who will provide a solution for the difficulties and problems which so many of them face in a strange land. He holds his 'surgeries' in the afternoon and they are attended by large numbers of people. The usual problems that he deals with are: (1) a wide variety of illnesses, especially female illnesses (2) unemployment (3) litigation (4) difficulties in personal relationships, especially between husband and wife, parent and child, brother and sister, friend and enemy. Curiously, problems arising from racism and racial attacks are seldom brought to him for solution.

His consultative method is to see clients individually: no-one may accompany anyone else. As in the case of A, the majority of his clients are women and others with little in the way of a British education. However, a number of young people of both sexes, who are British born and bred, also seek his advice.

Remedies also resemble those employed by A: charms worn on the body, or soaked in water, which is then drunk or sprinkled over the client's house; other charms tied to the ceiling or burnt in the corners of the house; indistinguishable verses recited; and blowing in the client's face.

B's minimum fee for one charm is £25 and his daily income runs into at least three figures. His is well-known among Muslim groups in both the Pakistani and Indian parts of the Punjab. Village rivalries, caste differences, sectarian fanaticism, and pure jealousy, aroused during efforts to gain importance and prestige in the Pakistani community, are some of the common divisive and stress-provoking social factors that exist among Pakistani groups in Britain. During the last five years there were occasions when physical violence and rioting occurred in the mosque, which had to be closed by the police.

B knows how to keep these issues alive. About eighteen months ago, when some people were killed in a road accident, differences within the community almost caused an outbreak of rioting over the funeral prayers for the dead. However, with the speedy arrival of the police, the situation was defused. Once again the Mavlana, without justification, was credited with the role of peacemaker. His influence on the community is tremendous.

A third practitioner, C, is an elderly man who has lived in England for many years. His children are all married to Pakistanis in this country, and — this is important! — his son and son-in-law run a grocer's shop near his home in a small town in the home counties. He is a poet, who writes in Urdu and Punjabi, and he has published collections of his work. In the last couple of years, however, he has become well-known for his supposed supernatural powers. He is known to members of the community by word of mouth, and advance appointments must be made in order to see him, otherwise a client may have to wait three or four months for his turn. C is engaged in the business on a full-time basis, and has no other job. Most of his clients are from the Punjab. While there is a wide age-range, from teenagers to advanced old age, the majority, who belong to different religions, are women, who come accompanied by parents or the men of their family.

C, who works seven days a week and charges £11 for a consultation, sees on average twenty to thirty clients a day. The most common problem is the relationship of parents with their children, particularly over marriage arrangements. Other recurring problems are: relationships between husbands and wives, relationships between brothers and sisters, illness, problems connected with failure in business, unemployment, fear of the jealousy and hatred of others, fear of witchcraft, fear of family interference in matrimonial affairs, and fear of relatives arising from this.

The most usual treatment prescribed by this practitioner are: (1) Presentation of charms. He has written many, which are stored in various cupboards. He selects a particular charm and then explains to the client what he should do with it. In cases of illness, the client has to soak the charm in water and drink the liquid, which is coloured by the ink used for the charm (2) The client may be asked to burn the charm at a particular spot in his house, or tie it to the main door of the house or a particular room (3) If a client complains about a son or daughter, the practitioner asks to be taken to the room where the child lives, to investigate the possibility of evil spirits. A lot of time and money may be needed so that he can travel to remote parts of Birmingham, Bradford, and London, for this purpose.

Sometimes he asks the client to go and bring a couple of pounds of almonds and dried dates. Usually the client says he cannot get these straight away and it will take some time to fetch them. But C sends them to the neighbouring shop, which is owned by his son and son-in-law. When the items have been purchased, he recites something, blows on the foodstuffs, and returns them to the client. He instructs them to eat the fruit and nuts every morning for two weeks, and report back. It is not easy to assess how many satisfied customers result from this treatment,

but the obvious continuity, and demands upon his business, testify to
this practitioner's popularity.

As we have seen, many of those who require such services are literate
and well-educated. Hence the newspaper agony aunt often features in
this role. Here are some examples from February of 1985:

(1) 'I wrote to you earlier, but didn't hear anything from you, and
I'm writing to you again. My problem is that I came to this country from
Pakistan about 5 years ago, and my husband was already living here. My
husband is white and red, like English people, whereas my colour is a
bit yellowish and blackish. When I see myself in the mirror sometimes I
feel terrified. Sometimes my husband remarks: 'Your colour is like men!'
And sometimes he says that your eyes are very low inside your face, and
your cheeks are rather heavily coming out.

'Now tell me I'm not at fault about my face and about my eyes. I
can't do anything. I've two children and by grace of God they're also
white and red like their father. Only I look different in the family. If
I could get my face a bit lighter and red, and become more attractive,
I would be grateful to you forever. The second problem is that when I
wear make-up my colour gets blacker.

'My husband becomes very angry very fast. When he visited Pakistan
last-time, since then he has changed a lot. In rage he says often 'I shall
divorce you and teach you a lesson!' This word divorce is like a poison
for me; but after a while he cools down and he's alright. I request you to
tell me some spiritual remedy, so that my husband should not get angry
and we should live happily. On my face there are some pock-marks as
well. Please tell me some remedy for that too.'

Reply: 'First in the morning make a cup of tea for your husband and
recite part of the Koran. Then blow in the cup before giving it to your
husband. For yourself, eat one apple every day, and drink milk.'[2]

(2) 'I think that somewhere somebody has done some evil eye on me. I
went to a spiritual person and he told me to get in touch with you. Now
please tell me how I can remedy the evil eye effect on me.'

Reply: 'After morning and night prayers, read once this part of the
Koran. Then blow on a glass of water and drink it. Do this for ninety
days.'[3]

(3) 'I wish to make you aware of my problems. I am being watched
so closely that I am afraid of writing to you. When I was in Pakistan my
aunt did not allow me to live happily and she did some charms on me,
so that I should run away from my home. Now I am in Britain. In spite
of that I see her in my dreams every night. I also see a large number of
stray dogs chasing me. When I see my aunt I get most terrified. I get
bad ideas sometimes. I feel aches and pains near my heart, and in the

evenings I begin to feel upset and unwell. I keep myself very clean and I'm a regular worshipper. I used to see even the Prophet and Medina in my dreams; but now I only have bad dreams. Recently I saw a dream in which I felt I was wearing a white thin material around me and I was flying towards the sky. Suddenly I awoke.'

Reply: 'After the night prayers read this part of the Koran. Secondly, go and seek guidance from a spiritual teacher. I find that there are faculties and capabilities which can be very useful for your spiritual development and upliftment.'[4]

(4) 'I have a son. Three times he failed in the examination. He says he tried hard, but still he fails; but I know he doesn't study much. He's very keen on roaming about; he never settles down. He doesn't accept what I say. If I say anything, he gets very angry. He's afraid of his father. All of his friends are Hindus and Sikhs. These days his girl-friend is also a Hindu. He's all alone in the house; perhaps that's why he doesn't settle down. This is rather a terrible state of affairs.'

Reply: 'When you son is sleeping at night, remain at a distance of one foot from him and read this part of the Koran. Don't wake him. Do it for 90 days.'[5]

(5) 'Dear Sir, I'm writing to you in real urgency. My problem is quite complicated. I got married about 10 years ago and I now have 2 children. We live at Southall. For the past few years my wife does not like me, and does not come near me at all, and she does not allow my children to come near me as well.

'She says I smell very foul. However, I wear perfumes. I heard from elders and from wise people — I also read it in books — that a man can get married to a fairy, so I'm writing, so you can tell me the way I should go about it. Any time of charm or suggestion procedure by your spiritual guide would be most helpful. I shall be very grateful to you.'

Reply: 'We really do not know any address of fairies. We would earnestly request you to tell us the names of books which describe the possibility of a man getting married to a fairy. That would be a great contribution to our knowledge and to the knowledge of our readers. However, we thank you for giving us the benefit of your personal experience on the subject.[6]

A final example of a practitioner — and here the circumstances permit me to provide full details — is interesting for a variety of reasons which will shortly become apparent, notably, because it illustrates the strong link that exists between the motherland and Great Britain in the minds of the immigrants. Haji Abdul Khaliq is better known by his popular name, Baba Jinnawala. Baba means 'grandfather', a term in Indian culture denoting respect, because an elderly man is symbolic of wisdom. He practises in Kasur, a town situated about thirty miles to the east of Lahore. It is linked with the noted Punjabi poet-saint, Balia Bulley Shah, who lived there in the mid-nineteenth century. The Punjab was at that time experiencing a period of great turbulence. Robbery, murder and general lawlessness were common then and fanaticism was rife. The poems of Bulley Shah, which he recited at mass meetings, opposed divisions of the people based on income, religion, and education. Indeed, he campaigned against all bigotry.

Bulley Shah was buried in Kasur. During his lifetime he had a large and popular following and, after his death, his reputation continued to grow, and his name became known throughout the Indian sub-continent. His poems have been set to Punjabi music, and are sung on radio and television. He himself is one of the most popular figures with Punjabis, whatever their religious beliefs. Every Thursday people come from far and wide to gather at his grave in Railway Road, where they pay homage and make offerings. It is a Moslem custom to visit graves on a Thursday, thought to be auspicious, because it is the day before Friday, the Islamic holy day. Hundreds of thousands gather for the anniversary of his death. An informant comments that: 'His philosophy adds richly to the development of mysticism. His life and death in Kasur contributed greatly to the history of saintly men'. Certainly he may be viewed as the forerunner and inspiration of Baba Jinnawala.

Kasur is an ancient town and, during the medieval period of Indian history, it made its mark as the seat of local rulers. After Abdul Samad, the last Moghul ruler, it was annexed to the Punjab Sikh State of Raja Ranjit Singh. In 1849 it became part of the British Empire, when Britain annexed the Punjab. A century and a quarter later, it was given the status of a separate district of Lahore Division.

Apart from Balia Bulley Shah, Kasur is noted for various eminent people, e.g. the singer and actress Noor Jehan, and Nawab Muhammad Ah Mad Khan. The former Prime Minister of Pakistan, Z. A. Bhutto, himself from Kasur, was accused of the murder of the Nawab, tried and hanged. Thus Kasur has both national and international significance, but it is not well-developed. There are only twenty-three large industrial units, consisting of chemical plant, food-processing, textiles and engineering works. The town is two and a half miles from the India-Pakistan border. These two countries have twice been at war, and traffic to India through Kasur is not allowed. Border clashes can be expected at any time, depending on the state of the relationship between the two countries, and the mood of the border troops. Thus, in spite of a long history of fame and importance, Kasur has not developed as it should have done. Instead people with wealth and skills move out, leaving only small businesses and farming communities. Life has remained virtually unchanged over the years, and educational and health services are insufficient to serve the population. According to the current District Census Report of Kasur District, there are 4 small Colleges of Further Education, 59 High Schools, and 2 hospitals with 79 beds, for a population of 1,528,002. Literacy is 18.7%.[7] This is despite the fact that Kasur is geographically close to Lahore, a highly developed city, with various educational facilities. Here, then, is the historico-socio-economic background against which the work and services of Haji Abdul Khaliq, alias Baba Jinnawala, should be viewed.

The Baba is well-known, not only as a Hakim — an Eastern physician and herbalist, practising traditional medicine — but, more importantly, for his work as a spiritualist. He was born in Kaloowala village in 1917. His schooling there consisted simply of some reading of Arabic from local evening classes, arranged by the Imam of the local mosque. He was engaged in tending sheep and goats. Then, at the age of 10, he took up the family occupation, farming. He states that it was hard work, but he found time in the evenings, and at night, to memorise and perform recitations of religious verses, including portions of the Koran. He visited the graves of a number of saints and holy people, e.g. Saint Golara, Sharakpur Sharif and Saint Haider Ali Shahi, and some of these individuals asked him not to continue with his efforts. But he proceeded with his studies, spending whole nights in holy recitations. Finally in 1960 he was in a position to set up his own healing durbar, or establishment, in the Bazaar at Kasur, near the road leading to the railway station. It is called Naya Bazaar, or Pottery Gate, and people come for spiritual guidance, blessing, and relief from physical illness and mental problems.

The accommodation consists of four rooms, a courtyard, lavatories, and washrooms. The flush-system lavatories and washrooms are for public use, and such facilities are provided nowhere else in the district. The Baba's main workrooms consist of an open verandah, where his sons and servants work and, inside, a big room, where he sits on a cushion. Through this big room one can see a large store full of medicines and pickles, and another room for spiritual diagnosis. A number of string-beds and sacks of chapati flour can also be seen. His own room is equipped with benches, bottles, and containers of herbal medicine. No appointment is needed to attend his 'clinic' and there is no charge. Everyone who comes is offered a free soft drink and a simple meal, and is given a one-rupee note. This is currently worth 4p but, in 1960, its value was a shilling.

Speaking about his work, the Baba explained that everyone who comes to see him has a problem or difficulty of some kind. Some are suffering from physical illness, others have economic problems. He treats them all with the help of Allah, from whom, he says, all assistance comes. He himself is only a kind of agent. He says all sorts of people come to him; some are rich, others are poor. Men, women, and children of all ages, every social background, and from far and wide, come to see him. He does not believe in, nor exercise, discrimination. People come, and he does not need to advertise. His fame springs from those who have been successfully treated, and it is passed on by word of mouth. He offers them, not only a simple free meal, but a bed for the night, if they wish to stay, and no charge is made for this service. The Baba does not have a bank account. People make offerings and he spends a great deal on the maintenance of his services, on a local school, and on various charities, which provide help for the poor. He also supports several Islamic schools and helps to pay for his clients' funeral arrangements.

His staff consists of his three sons: Haji Muhammed Umar Tabassum, aged 33; Muhammed Luqman, aged 27; and Muhammed Husain, aged 23; as well as two servants, Maulvi Muhammed Rafiqie, aged 39, and Hakim Abdul Razaque, aged 50. In addition Khalid Mahmud often acts as correspondence secretary.

The clinic is open from sunrise to sunset. In the evening the Baba is invited out to dinner by clients. He combines these visits with treatment and diagnosis of disease and spiritual ailments, and his hosts on these occasions invariably pay him hundreds of rupees. Some may live as far away as Rawalpindi — 210 miles from Kasur — and they will send a car to fetch him, and to transport him back after the meal.

His clients consist of: (1) those rejected by doctors and hospitals, or suffering from post-operation complications (2) childless couples (3) cases of spiritual possession and haunting by evil spirits (4) those who have lost their property (5) those who have lost members of their families through death (6) victims of robbery and violence (7) sufferers from hysteria and nervous disorders (8) those wishing to promote their business interests, or seeking jobs (9) those experiencing domestic problems, conflicts, and violence (10) people involved in litigation (11) people involved in marriage arrangements, or experiencing marital problems (12) election candidates (13) the mentally ill (14) the poor. The average number of clients is over a hundred a day, seven days a week. To date, the Baba claims to have attended well over a million.

The statistical breakdown of the daily average of a hundred clients is as follows: (1) 25%–30% are men; 70%–75% are women (2) 55% come from rural areas; 45% from an urban background (3) 80% are illiterate; 20% literate (4) 60% are 17–35 year-olds; 40% are over 35 (5) 75%–80% are poor; 20%–25% are wealthy. Thus a picture emerges of a majority of poor, illiterate, young women, the most disadvantaged group in this society, as so often elsewhere. However, it is interesting that the proportion of literate clients is slightly higher than the literacy rate of the local population.

On average, out of the Baba's hundred daily patients, 80% are just suffering from fatigue, rejection, poverty, dejection, and frustration. He listens to each and acts as a confidant, praying, and offering them charms and herbal medicine. The other 20% are supposed to be suffering from possession by spirits, and these he takes into his spiritual consultation room. He lights his earthen lamp, and asks one of the boys working for him to look at the light. He recites a text from the Koran, and then asks the child to diagnose the patient's problems, their causes, and origins. Next the Baba takes his rod and beats the client, until the evil spirit has departed. The usual methods he uses for treatment are: (1) The hot knife process. This involves drawing a hot knife across the patient's back. The flesh is burnt, but no-one ever complains. (2) The patient is caught by the leg and shaken violently (3) The patient's hair is twisted and pulled very hard (4) The patient is slapped. (5) The patient inhales thick smoke from burning herbs, while the Baba recites portions of the Koran.

Grateful patients show their appreciation in many ways. They return bringing gifts of money, clothing, sweets, fruit, and various cooked and uncooked foodstuffs. The Baba is often invited to visit other parts of the country. He was also requested to make the pilgrimage to Mecca and the cost, about £2,500, was paid by a former patient. One of his sons was invited to Britain for a month as a guest, proceeding afterwards to Mecca as a pilgrim. Usually this is for three weeks, but he stayed for a month.

A great many Asians write to the Baba from Great Britain, the United States, Canada, West Germany, and France. They consult him about their problems, which consist of family friction, unemployment, and illness. Some confide in him their feelings of strangeness in the West. He sends them charms and suggests ways of coping with their difficulties, which include prayer. Some of these remedies are successful, and clients send him money, in some cases hundreds of pounds. Some are willing to pay for his staff and members of his family to visit the West. Recently, when his son came to Britain for a month, the entire expenses of his visit were borne by one family. This was because they had been having difficulties with their daughter-in-law, who filed a suit against them. She also wanted a divorce, and this was their wish too. They had written to the Baba, asking for help, and he sent charms, and prayed for them. The divorce was granted by the court, but the other cases were rejected. In gratitude, the family entertained the Baba's son as their guest, at an estimated cost of £3,500. During this visit, the young man became well-known among the Asian community in London, and the Baba himself acquired many new clients by correspondence.

The Baba's room in Kasur is full of certificates and letters of appreciation from patients. These include: (1) A leading industrialist (2) A major in the Pakistan army (3) The Secretary General of the Pakistan People's Party (4) A member of the Royal Cabinet of the Kingdom of Saudi Arabia (5) Members of the Provincial Assembly, and the National Assembly. In an area noted for religious dissension, his patients include Christians, Hindus and Sikhs, as well as Moslems. His overseas clients include Sikhs and Hindus in Britain, Canada and India. Here are two sample letters, written by government officials:

(1) 'To whom it may concern. This is to certify that I personally know Hakim Maulvi Abdul Khaliq of Naya Bazaar, Kasur, for the last several years. He is an efficient Hakim, and a zealous spiritualist. He is an honest, pious, and religious person, of great human virtues. He is serving suffering humanity through spiritual means free of cost, and charges only for medicines, if and when, given. To the best of my knowledge he does not indulge in fraud, or exploitation of the people who come to him for treatment and sprititual guidance — (Signed) Aziz Ahmed Saddique. Section Officer, Police, Home Dept, Lahore.'

(2) 'I, Muhammed Sharif, Overseer, Public Works Dept, Lahore, hereby certify that my nephew Muhammed Akram was tried by the Martial Law authorities in Lahore, and was ordered to be hanged. I approached the Baba and he prayed for us, and gave me charms. There were only three days left before the scheduled execution. Suddenly all the orders of the Martial Law authorities were cancelled. Thus my nephew was saved from the gallows. I believe it was through the spiritual efforts of Baba Jinnawala.'

An informant commented: 'It is clear that much of the Baba's treatment is designed to supply psychological needs in his patients, among them those of the schizophrenic, who hears voices, or sees visions, interpreted as 'haunting' or 'possession'. Physical suffering, through beating, burning etc., is a common primitive treatment for such cases, and it is only comparatively recently that psychiatric knowledge in the West has developed more humane methods of dealing with such disorders. Those obsessed with guilt, real or perceived, may also seek a form of suffering, and this the Baba supplies. Flagellation can also represent a form of sexual perversion, and it is interesting that only those who offer themselves for beating, receive this particular treatment. It may be worth noting that, to carry out such treatment, and other methods of torture masquerading as treatment, demands a certain type of personality in the inflictor, and the attitudes and activities of the Baba himself would provide fertile investigative ground for a psychologist. Intensive private investigation by an anthropologist, of patients, both those who receive benefit, and those who do not, would reveal much on how reputations of healers are built up, including such factors as need, suggestibility, popular opinion, bribery, threat, and fear, as well as gratitude, and admiration'. His personal opinion is that the services of the Baba are genuinely appreciated, and that no element of deceit or fraud is involved. The Baba himself remarked (April 10th 1986) to him that: '50% of the people will be cured, whether they come to me or not'.

In a paper as short as this, it has only been possible for me to refer very briefly to these few examples, selected from fieldwork. Even so, one is struck by the religious element in the work of these practitioners. One is an Imam, a second decorates his home lavishly, and conspicuously, with beautifully inscribed quotations from the Koran. Remedies include religious incantations, and reading portions from the Muslim holy book. Traditionally Muslims regard religious incantations with great respect. They are thought capable of rewarding individuals on spiritual, mental, and physical levels. They are also thought to possess great potential for evil, if used to gratify a selfish desire.

Ishwaran has written: 'In a developing (area) like (the) Indian sub-continent, where the social security system is still largely inadequate, the extended kinship network functions as a social insurance agency, assisting in education, employment, sickness, widowhood, old age (and so forth). Hence, the individual and the elementary family often cannot thrive independently, and this helplessness is dramatised in times of distress and crisis, when the interdependence among relatives, even though living apart residentially, is reinforced. In (the) Indian sub-continent the traditional extended family still exists as a functional unit in most ways, except residentially. At the international level, practically every elementary family is closely dependent on its extended kinship configuration, for all its major activities'.[8]

Problems within the family network are intensified by the immigrant situation in Britain, particularly for women, who often lack the benefits of education. The strains that occur in these personal relationships are magnified by many factors: for example, the greater emancipation of British women, and all that this implies with regard to the position of both older Asian women, and the new generation. These, and related problems and conflicts, are the cause of much distress, which in turn creates a rich source of income for practitioners of magic, witchcraft, and the supernatural. The more unscrupulous may enlist the help of religious belief to strengthen their position.

NOTES

1. *The Compact Edition of the Oxford Dictionary* (Oxford, 1971), II, 395.
2. Firdaus Kamar, 9th February 1985, *Jang*, Shams-ud-dan-Azimee.
3. Farooq, Preston, 4th February 1985, *Jang*.
4. Mrs Khan, Preston, 4th February 1985, *Jang*.
5. Mrs Farrukh Begum, 4th February 1985, *Jang*.
6. Muhammad Nazir, Southall, 4th February 1985, *Jang*.
7. *Population Census Report*, No. 55, 3–5.
8. K. Ishwaran, 'Interdependence of the Elementary and Extended Family', ed. John S. Augustine, *The Indian Family in Transition* (Delhi, 1982), 21.